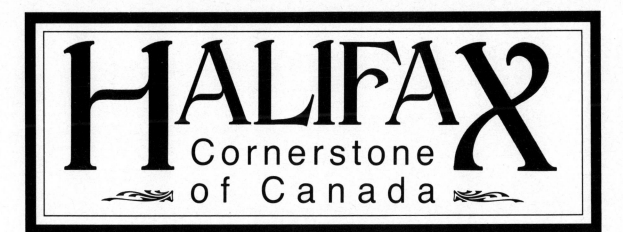

Picture Research
by David MacLaren

Partners in Progress
by John P. Mason

Produced in cooperation with
the Halifax Board of Trade

Windsor Publications

HALIFAX
Cornerstone
of Canada

 Joan M. Payzant

Windsor Publications, Inc.—History Book Division

Publisher: John M. Phillips
Editorial Director: Teri Davis Greenberg
Design Director: Alexander D'Anca

Staff for *Halifax: Cornerstone of Canada*
Senior Editor: Michelle Hudun
Editorial Development: Lynn Kronzek
Director, Corporate Biographies: Karen Story
Assistant Director, Corporate Biographies: Phyllis Gray
Editor, Corporate Biographies: Judith Hunter
Editorial Assistants: Kathy M. Brown, Marilyn
   Horn, Lonnie Pham, Pat Pittman, Lane A.
   Powell, Sharon Volz
Designer: J.R. Vasquez
Text Layout Artist: Susan L. Wells
Corporate Biographies Layout Artist: Mari Preimesberger

Advisory Committee:
Hon. John M. Buchanan, Q.C.
Dr. A. Gordon Archibald
Louis R. Comeau
Richard L. Criddle
Dr. E. Margaret Fulton
David B. Hyndman
J. Keith Lawton
Dr. W. Andrew MacKay
Ian C. MacLellan
J. Rod McLeod
Charles A. Marshall
Ralph M. Medjuck
C. Arnie Patterson
Robert P. Radchuck, C.A.
Gavin J. Rainnie
Henry B. Rhude
George B. Robertson, Q.C.
Allan C. Shaw
George C. Thompson
Vice-Admiral J.C. Wood

First Edition
ISBN 0-89781-149-6

Endpapers
This detail from Robert
Wilkie's circa 1860 oil
painting of *Halifax Harbour from Windmill Pier Dartmouth* illustrates the
town's continuing military role in the affairs of
the British empire. Please
see page 105 to view this
painting in full colour.
From the Collection of
the Art Gallery of Nova
Scotia

CONTENTS

PREFACE

It is a long-felt public want . . . to
point out to the World . . . how
the peerless Port of Halifax—the
Indian "Chebucto or Great Harbour" of immemorial legend—had
been fashioned by Nature to become indirectly the Corner Stone
of Canada, of a revamped Empire
and of British Democracy
Overseas.

From *1,000 Facts about Halifax, Nova Scotia*
by John Quinpool (John Regan), 1943

Since 1803 the Old Town
Clock has been a remind-
er of the stay of Edward,
Duke of Kent, in Halifax.
A military man from the
word go, the Duke had
the clock installed to
keep both town and garri-
son punctual. Courtesy,
Precision Photographic
Services

ACKNOWLEDGMENTS

I would like to thank the staff of the Public Archives of Nova Scotia for the help they gave me in researching material for this book, particularly Mr. Allan Dunlop, Acting Provincial Archivist, and Mr. John MacLeod, Public Records Archivist. To Dr. Phyllis Blakeley, CM, Provincial Archivist for Nova Scotia (retired, 1985), I owe a special debt of gratitude for her reading of the manuscript and invaluable suggestions for its improvement.

Mr. Patrick Laurette, Assistant Curator of the Art Gallery of Nova Scotia, not only provided me with useful information, but generously gave of his time to answer my questions about artists in Halifax.

Captain Donald R. Snider of the Halifax Fire Department Headquarters was very helpful in telling me of modern methods of fire fighting and fire prevention.

To these and others who helped in many ways, my sincere thanks.

Joan M. Payzant,
Dartmouth, Nova Scotia
September 1985

The MacDonald Bridge, opened in April 1955, was named in honour of Angus L. MacDonald, a former Nova Scotia Premier. The toll bridge is 1.5 kilometers in length and upon its completion, after three years of construction, was the second longest suspension bridge in the Commonwealth.
Photo by John C. Davie

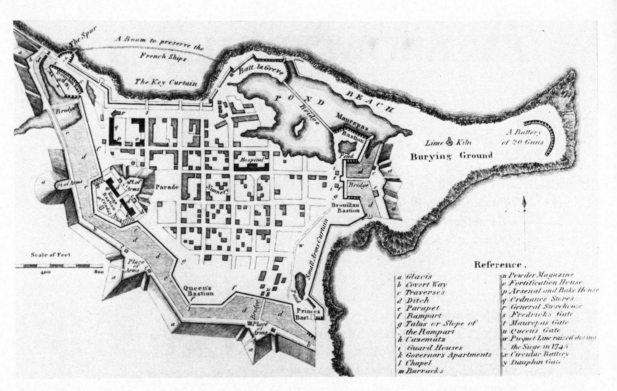

Once the keystone of defending France's North American colonies, Louisbourg's fate was pivotal to the history of a continent. In large measure the establishment of Halifax was a response to this symbol of French power. This *Plan of the Town of Louisbourg* was drawn by C.W. Torbett. From the Collection of the Art Gallery of Nova Scotia

C H A P T E R   I

THE STRUGGLE FOR POSSESSION

Each summer the nomadic Micmac Indians, a tribe of the Algonquin nation, paddled their light birchbark canoes down the rivers that led to the great harbour of Chebooktook. On its shores they set up their conical wigwams and began their summer way of life—fishing, clam digging, and berry picking. For centuries the Micmacs were undisturbed by the presence of the white man as they followed this seasonal pattern, returning to the shelter of the forest in the autumn for the good hunting it afforded.

Toward the end of the fifteenth century, however, explorers from Europe began their adventurous journeys westward, and by 1604 at least thirty different explorers are thought to have touched the little peninsula that was to become Nova Scotia. One such explorer, Giovanni da Verrazano, named the east coast of North America "Arcadia." Variations of this name have appeared on maps through the years as Arcadia, Acadie, and Acadia.

The first colony of any permanence in Acadia was founded in 1604 by Pierre du Gast, Sieur de Monts, who planted the French flag on the shore of the Bay of Fundy at the western end of the peninsula. Today a life-size replica of the sturdy wooden Habitation, a community-in-miniature and fort combined, is a reminder of the structure built for that early settlement.

With the Sieur de Monts was Samuel Champlain, geographer and navigator, who ventured forth from the Habitation to map out the surrounding coastline. In 1607 Champlain came to Chebooktook and described it as "a very safe bay." Another French visitor in 1693, calling it "Schibouctou," said that the harbour was the best in all of Acadia and New England as well. These words of praise led to the establishment of a French fishing company at the great harbour, but it was short-lived. In 1711 De Labat, a French military engineer, made a detailed plan of the harbour and estimated that, along with the large basin beyond, it could easily hold over 1,000 vessels.

A recent picture of the
Fortress of Louisbourg
illustrates the fact that it
is still one of the wonders
of the world—especially
to tourists. Courtesy, The
Image Farm

In spite of these glowing descriptions
of the great harbour of Chebucto, as it
came to be known, it was never settled
by the French. Port Royal remained the
most prominent settlement in Acadia for
well over 100 years.

The people of New England and Virginia were not happy about a French settlement so close to their shores, and in
1613 Captain Samuel Argall of Virginia
attacked and burned the Habitation.
This marked the beginning of the seesaw
struggle between French and English for
domination of Acadia.

In terms of the province's later history
the most significant of the British settlements at Port Royal was that of a Scot,
Sir William Alexander. Alexander con-
ceived a brilliant scheme to raise money
for a colony there, to be named New
Scotland. Any Scotsman who coveted a
title could be made a Knight Baronet of
New Scotland by paying 166 pounds for
the privilege, and the proceeds were to go
toward establishing the colony. King
James I granted the charter for the new

colony, and its name, written on the
charter in formal Latin, was "Nova
Scotia."

The knighting ceremony took place at
Edinburgh Castle on May 28, 1625. Nu-
merous Scots flocked there to be dubbed
Knights Baronets of Nova Scotia. Nova
Scotia's distinguished coat of arms and
flag also date from this period, long-
lasting symbols of a temporary settlement. Today a plaque near the entrance
of Edinburgh Castle commemorates the
grand scheme for the founding of a New
Scotland across the Atlantic.

In 1632 Acadia returned once more to
French occupation. In the years to come
new settlers were brought in to live in
the surrounding area. Here they developed prosperous farms in the Annapolis
Valley. Marshland was reclaimed by dik-
ing, a technique they had learned in their
native France. In 1710 the fort was captured for the last time by the English,
and Port Royal was renamed Annapolis
Royal in honour of Queen Anne. Through
the Treaty of Utrecht all the mainland of

Acadia was given to the British, but the French still held the two islands that today are called Prince Edward Island and Cape Breton Island.

Determined to hold these two possessions and guard the entrance to the Saint Lawrence in order to protect Quebec, Montreal, and other small settlements along the river, the French immediately began to construct the great Fortress of Louisbourg on Ile Royale (Cape Breton today). Even in the eighteenth century Louisbourg was one of the wonders of the world, a walled city of 5,000 people—ordinary citizens, naval and military personnel, and traders and fishermen from Europe and New England. It was a cosmopolitan port, thriving on trade and full of activity.

Acadians from mainland Nova Scotia carried on an illegal trade with Louisbourg—vegetables, grain, pigs, sheep, and cattle in exchange for goods from France. New Englanders were also lured by this sophisticated outpost of France, but while they looked with awe at its facilities, they were aware of its military might.

Small Fort Anne on the Nova Scotia mainland stood as the only defense between Louisbourg and New England. Six times French from Quebec aided by Indians attacked it, determined to regain control of Acadia. Fortunately Paul Mascarene, Governor of Nova Scotia, stationed at Annapolis Royal (the old capital), was popular with the Acadians. Because he was firm and just and could speak French they supported him and helped to defend the fort.

Worried by the double threat of French attacks overland from Quebec or by sea from Louisbourg, New Englanders were determined to capture the great fortress. All able-bodied men joined forces under militia Colonel William Pepperell and set sail for Louisbourg with 100 ships. They were joined at Canso by three British warships under Commodore Warren.

Due to sheer determination on the New Englanders' part and the Frenchmen's overconfidence, combined with poor preparation for such an attack, the New Englanders captured Louisbourg after bombarding it for forty-nine days. By then all those inside the walls were starving and many had been wounded or killed.

Even though they had won the battle the New Englanders had a wretched winter ahead of them. They were not allowed to go home to their families because they were forced to guard the once mighty fortress. They drank too much rum and nearly 1,000 of them became ill and died during the long winter.

When the news that Louisbourg had been captured reached France, a huge fleet of sixty-five warships was sent across the Atlantic under the Duc d'Anville. His plans were to recapture Louisbourg and to take all British territory along the coast.

As though it had been cursed, d'Anville's fleet met with disaster after disaster—storms, shipwrecks, and disease. Sable Island, known as the graveyard of the Atlantic, claimed some of the fleet and the remaining ships were blown off course and put in to Chebucto. There, in the basin at the far end of the harbour, Duc d'Anville died, as did dozens of others. These men were buried on the shores of the Basin and it is said that Indians who retrieved the discarded uniforms of the French were infected with their diseases, causing hundreds of deaths in Micmac villages during the following winter.

As for the great French fleet, some of the ships were scuttled on the eastern side of the basin at Chebucto, and the few remaining ships straggled sadly back to France.

When war ended between France and England in 1748, the Treaty of Aix-la-Chapelle was signed. New Englanders who had fought so hard to capture Louisbourg were stunned to learn that one of the terms of the treaty gave Louisbourg back to the French. New Englanders were furious at the British for this blatant disregard of their struggle and hard-won victory. To add to their rage, they

were required to remain at Louisbourg
until the French were able to gather replacements and a fleet of transports to
bring them across the Atlantic. France
had decided to rebuild Louisbourg, making it stronger than ever, once again leaving Annapolis Royal and New England in
a very vulnerable position. This high-
handed decision by the British government caused strong resentment in New
England, sowing seeds of anger that finally bloomed during the American Revolution.

Later Governor William Shirley of
Massachusetts, one of the prime instiga-
tors behind the New England capture of
Louisbourg, spoke out strongly in favour
of establishing a permanent British colony somewhere on the Atlantic coast of
Nova Scotia and of encouraging English-
speaking people to emigrate. His recom-
mendations were finally heeded by the
British government, and under the auspices of George Dunk Montague, Lord
Halifax, President of the Board of Trade
and Plantations, advertisements were
placed in English newspapers encourag-

ing people to emigrate. Lord Halifax gave
special incentives to disbanded soldiers
and seamen because he said they were
"men of tried courage and loyalty, inured
to hardships, accustomed to enterprises
of difficulty and danger, familiarized to
subordination, and willing to obey orders."

A location on the shore of Chebucto
harbour was chosen as the site for the
new settlement, for as Otis Little, an attorney, wrote:

*It [Chebucto] has a short and easy com-
munication by land with all the settlements on the Bay of Fundy, is equally
commodious for the fishery with Canso,
and is more in the way of all ships passing
to and from Europe to New England that
may occasionally or by stress of weather
seek a port for shelter or relief. Its Harbour gives place to none in the world,
and by its natural form, and an island at
its entrance, is capable of being well de-
fended by a regular fortification.*

The Honourable Edward Cornwallis,

uncle of Lord Charles Cornwallis who surrendered at Yorktown in 1781 (the British defeat that ended the fighting in the American Revolution) was appointed Captain General and Governor-in-Chief of the expedition. In the sloop-of-war *Sphinx* he sailed from England on May 14, 1749, to take over his new command, with instructions to report his progress to the Duke of Bedford, Secretary of State.

On June 22, 1749, having arrived at Chebucto, Cornwallis wrote:

My Lord Duke: . . . I can give your Grace little information as yet as to this country—the coasts are as rich as ever they have been represented. We caught fish every day since we came within fifty leagues of the coast, the harbour itself is full of fish of all kinds; all the officers agree the harbour is the finest they have ever seen. The country is one continual wood, no clear spot to be seen or heard of. I have been ashore in several places— the underwood is only young trees so that with difficulty one might walk through any of them; D'Anville's fleet have only cut wood for present use, but cleared no ground, they encamped their men upon the beach. I have seen but few brooks nor have as yet found the naviga- ble river that has been talked of. There are a few French families on the east side of the bay about three leagues off; some have been on board. As to the disposition of the French or Indians I can give your Grace no account till I see Colonel Mascarene, when I shall write more fully and continue from time to time to ac- quaint Your Grace of our proceedings. I wish the French may not be uneasy at waiting so long on board for the evacua- tion of Louisbourg as it may be some time before Mr. Hopson will get trans- ports—it will, I fear, retard the settle- ment.

I am &c., Ed. Cornwallis
P.S. I expect the transports daily.

The reference to Mr. Hopson was an in- teresting one. Peregrine Thomas Hopson

was the English Governor at Louisbourg at the time of the Treaty of Aix-la-Chapelle, and apparently was under the impression that the transports that were bringing the new settlers to Chebucto would be sent to Louisbourg to remove him and his troops. Meanwhile the French replacements had arrived from France and were cooped up in Louisbourg Harbour aboard ships. There was still no sign of empty British transports. Hopson was in an embarrassing predicament and Governor Cornwallis was very aware of the problem. It was one of many that he undertook to solve in the busy days that lay ahead.

Somewhere out on the Atlantic behind the *Sphinx*, thirteen British transports carrying about 2,500 passengers were also destined for Chebucto. Many of the passengers were discharged soldiers or sailors, who, unable to find work back home in England, had jumped at the chance of a free passage to Nova Scotia, free food for a year, their own land, arms and ammunition, materials and tools for building homes, and the equipment necessary for earning a living in their chosen occupations.

The voyage had been a fairly comfortable one, since the ships were equipped with ventilators to prevent air from stagnating. Only one small child had died during the crossing.

As soon as the vessels arrived, passengers were disembarked from six of them and put ashore on George's Island and given temporary shelter there. Governor Cornwallis then sent the empty ships on new missions. The *Fair Lady* went to Annapolis Royal, the old capital, to bring Governor Paul Mascarene and a quorum of his council to the new capital, Halifax—its name chosen to honour the Earl of Halifax, President of the Board of Trade in England, the sponsor of the expedition. The five other transports were dispatched to Louisbourg to pick up Governor Hopson and his troops, who were about to be replaced by the French regiments that were presently confined to their ships in Louisbourg Harbour and

impatiently waiting to reclaim the fortress.

Governor Cornwallis had already been ashore several times when the settlers arrived, and he had selected a site for the new town. He wrote to the Board of Trade:

From seeing the place only, one would be apt to choose Sandwich Point as the best situation for a town, being very defensible and having the advantage of Sandwich River, [now known as the Northwest Arm] navigable a great way. This was the general opinion at first, and they began to clear there, the first day they worked, but upon examination we found the strongest objections against it.

However unsuitable the site was for the new town, it became one of its greatest assets many years later as the recreation area called Point Pleasant Park.

A second site was then chosen further up the western shore, with a deep anchorage in front. John Bruce, an engineer, and Charles Morris, a surveyor, laid out the streets for the new town. These were fifty-five-feet wide and extended from the shoreline up a gradual slope to the foot of a high hill that protected the town from north winds. The most southerly street was Salter Street, and Buckingham the most northerly. Cross streets divided the town into blocks, and each block contained sixteen town lots.

On August 8, heads of families gathered to draw for their lots. Single men grouped together in fours and nominated one to be their head. The results of the draw were registered in an allotment book, which today can be seen on microfilm at the Public Archives of Nova Scotia.

The settlement immediately became a frantically busy place with the erection of wharves and storehouses, private homes, and public buildings. Supplies came each day from New England, and some of its merchants eventually moved to Halifax, seeing an opportunity for expanding their businesses. Cows and sheep were provided by the Acadians, and as soon as land

A recreation of the days at Louisbourg is illustrated in this contemporary photograph. Courtesy, the Image Farm

was cleared grain and vegetables were planted.

Cornwallis wrote to the Lords of Trade, "The number of active men proper to undertake and carry on a new settlement is very small. Of soldiers there are only 100, of tradesmen, sailors and others able and willing to work not above 200." Many of the settlers quickly drifted away on the New England schooners to more established settlements where they would not have to work so hard. They had no training in fending for themselves under ideal conditions, let alone trying to survive in this heavily wooded and rocky wilderness with the threat of winter hanging over them.

Worse than any of these problems was the danger of attack by the Indians and the French. First indications had been that both would be friendly to the English settlers. Indian chiefs came and signed treaties, the Acadians sent men to

help build a road to Minas and assist with construction at Halifax. One man sent to Acadia in 1737 under the auspices of the Foreign Missions at Paris changed all of this. He was the infamous Abbé Le Loutre, a "determined enemy of British rule," according to historian Duncan Campbell. He used the Indians to intercept messages from the government at Halifax to smaller settlements at Annapolis and Canso, and planned bloody massacres on the residents of these places.

There were no serious Indian attacks on Halifax itself but the London *Gentlemen's Magazine* of August 1750 had the following report:

Mr. Brown, gardener to Governor Cornwallis, with his son and four others, going out two or three miles from the town, were beset by the Indians, who killed him and his son, the latter they buried, but the other body was found on the ground scalped, and brought hither and buried; the four others, it is feared are killed or carried off.

A similar incident was related in a letter from a Halifax settler on October 2, 1749:

About seven o'clock on Saturday morning before, as several of Major Gilman's workmen with one soldier, unarmed were hewing sticks of timber about 200 yards from his house and mills on the east side of the harbour, [later, Dartmouth] they were surprised by about forty Indians, who first fired two shots and then a volley upon them which killed four, two of whom they scalped, and cut off the heads of the others. The fifth is missing and is supposed to have been carried off.

The French, urged on by Abbé Le Loutre, encouraged the Indians by paying for each English scalp turned in to them. The English were no better for, in retaliation, they offered rewards up to fifty pounds for Indian scalps. Two men, John Connor and James Grace, brought six scalps into Halifax after a bloody encounter with a group of Indians near Canso, during which two of their party had also been scalped.

Le Loutre urged the Acadians to refuse to sign the Oath of Allegiance, and persuaded them to take part in skirmishes against the English whenever possible. He travelled throughout the province stirring up trouble—now in Louisbourg, now in Chignecto, and further afield in Quebec and Paris. While the Bishop of Quebec condemned Le Loutre for meddling in temporal affairs and causing discontent among his parishioners, the military authorities in Quebec and Louisbourg supported his determined efforts to drive the British out of Nova Scotia.

The only way Cornwallis could at first persuade men to build defenses around Halifax was to pay them one shilling, six pence a day. After hearing of some of the Indian atrocities, the work of putting up a log palisade interspersed with wooden

forts right around the town was speeded up considerably. A thirty-foot-wide corridor immediately outside the palisade was cleared of trees to prevent Indians from hiding in the woods.

Frames and special planks were ordered from New England for two churches planned for the town and the governor's house. By October, Governor Cornwallis was able to move into his one-story house, built on the site of the present Province House.

By late autumn 300 houses had been finished, but a few settlers still lived on the transports or on George's Island throughout that first winter.

In 1750, late in the summer, 353 settlers arrived on the ship *Alderney* and were given land on the opposite side of the harbour near the original sawmill. This eventually became the town of Dartmouth. A blockhouse was built there, manned each night by a sergeant and about a dozen soldiers. In May 1751, however, there was a second Indian massacre and "the whole town was a scene of butchery," as one settler wrote back to London. Except for a small boy who rolled under his parents' bed, most of the settlers were murdered and their screams were heard across Halifax.

Three hundred German settlers came in September 1751 on the ship *Ann,* and new lots were laid out for them to the north of the original town of Halifax. Additional Germans and foreign Protestants arrived in 1751 and 1752, some of them being sent to Dartmouth to build a palisade around the small settlement there, and some to what is still called Dutch Village Road. Fifteen hundred of these Germans left in 1753 to form a settlement on the south shore of the province, which they named Lunenburg. This move considerably depleted the population of Halifax.

Governor Cornwallis and his successor, Hopson, had very short terms of office, and in 1755 Governor Charles Lawrence, a military man, was appointed to the position. Governor Lawrence was determined that the Acadians must take the

Oath of Allegiance, being alarmed at their close connections with the French military forts at Beauséjour and Louisbourg. As the first step in making the Acadians aware that the mainland of Nova Scotia would never again be under French control, Governor Lawrence decided to capture Fort Beauséjour. This was speedily accomplished with the French surrendering after one British shell destroyed a prison at the fort. One of the interesting aspects of this victory was that none other than the evil Le Loutre was inside the fort at the time. In his wily way he escaped from the British by slipping out of Fort Beauséjour in disguise and fled to Quebec where he was not welcomed. He left by ship for his native France, but justice caught up with him when the ship was captured by a Royal Navy ship. Le Loutre was kept as a British prisoner until 1763—the end of the Seven Years' War.

Meanwhile in Halifax, Governor Lawrence had made the difficult decision to expel the Acadians from their farmlands in the Annapolis Valley. For years they had refused to sign the Oath of Allegiance to the British, and this fact coupled with their obvious sympathy for the French at Louisbourg and Quebec made them a dangerous faction in the event of a full scale war with France. The resulting expulsion and scattering of the Acadians up and down the coast of the thirteen colonies was a black day in Nova Scotia's history, but deemed a necessity at the time. It is interesting to speculate on how different the outcome might have been if Le Loutre had encouraged the Acadians and Indians to live peacefully under British rule instead of inciting them to rebellion.

Governor Lawrence did not have much time to devote to the little settlement of Halifax, because of his greater involvement with affairs of the whole province. In 1758 a deluge of military and naval men arrived at Halifax under Sir Jeffrey Amherst and Admiral Edward Boscawen, determined to put an end to the French fortress at Louisbourg. Twenty-three ships of the line, eighteen frigates, and more than 100 transports were assembled in the harbour.

Living conditions in Halifax under the stress of such a sudden population explosion were far from ideal. The liquor outlets on the waterfront, the brothels at the upper levels of the town on Barrack Street, and the merchants as well prospered and did a thriving business, but the civilians suffered from shortages of supplies and were often terrorized by unruly mobs of soldiers and sailors.

Admiral Boscawen's fleet did not remain long in the harbour, but set sail for Louisbourg on May 28, 1758. After a two-month siege Louisbourg fell to the British for the last time.

The following year the Naval Yard (or Dockyard), with its careening yard, mast house, sail loft, and high shear-legs for raising masts, was officially opened along the northern shore of the harbour. Today, with many modifications, the Dockyard is still in active service. Admiralty House, built of local ironstone in 1814, served as the residence for the Commander-in-Chief of the North American and West Indies station. In 1819 Bermuda replaced Halifax as headquarters, and from then until 1904 Admiralty House was used as a summer residence only.

Since 1904 it has served as a hospital, officer's mess, library, and now as the Maritime Command Museum.

The Dockyard was turned over to the Canadian government by the Royal Navy in 1906 and was of immense importance during the two World Wars as the Royal Canadian Navy grew to be the third largest Allied fleet.

In 1759 Halifax saw the assemblage of another large force for the attack on Quebec, under the command of General James Wolfe. There was great rejoicing when the final defeat of the French in Canada was announced, while at the same time the death of young General Wolfe was mourned.

Being in the midst of the military and naval presence did not appeal to many of the settlers of Halifax and they were constantly leaving for more peaceful surroundings. By 1757 the population was only half of its original size, but whatever its failings as a colony, Halifax had excelled in its role as a naval port and military outpost. "To its position . . . may be ascribed in a great measure the downfall of the French power in America," wrote Dr. T.B. Akins, one of Halifax's early historians.

In 1761 and 1762 the chiefs of the various tribes of Indians throughout Nova Scotia came to Halifax to meet with government officials over new peace treaties. The last of these was attended with great ceremony. The treaty was signed by Chief Joseph Argunault and Governor Jonathan Belcher, and witnessed by members of Council, the speaker of the Assembly and Abbé Maillard, a Roman Catholic priest. The Indians washed off their war paint and buried a symbolic hatchet in the governor's garden just west of St. Paul's cemetery on what is now Spring Garden Road.

The conflict between the English and the Indians had ended, but trouble stirring in the colonies to the south threatened to embroil Halifax in a new upheaval.

In 1928 the Canadian government set Louisbourg aside as a National Historic Site. Interest in Louisbourg was sparked again in 1961 when the federal government instigated a program to restore part of the fortress to its eighteenth-century appearance. Photo by Esther Mugar. Courtesy, SF Photo Network

This 1801 view of Halifax from George's Island, looking WNW toward the Citadel, is reproduced from a coloured aquatint by George Isham Parkyns. From the Photograph Collection of the Public Archives of Nova Scotia

count of a man being flogged through the fleet in the harbour:

There were seven ships and he received a portion of his punishment on each ship. I stood on a wharf and saw the hammock in which he lay hoisted and lowered at each ship, and my heart sickened at the thought of his sufferings. Three days after, he died in the hospital, but whether from the flogging or other cause I did not learn.

A little girl of ten witnessed an even more horrifying spectacle in 1844. Mrs. P.H. Lenoir related in her memoirs that her father took her to watch the executions of four men convicted of murder in the famous *Saladin* piracy case. The execution took place on the grounds of the present Victoria General Hospital:

The big open space was crowded with people. A procession was coming up Tower Road—troops of soldiers, two closed cars, the sheriff in his gig, more soldiers. It was the prisoners being brought from the Penitentiary on the shores of the Arm. The four condemned men stepped out of the prison wagon—all of them were young men—the oldest not more than twenty-two or twenty-three. They were dressed in black with white shirts. Each man had a coil of rope round his arm, the other end of which was knotted around his neck. One of the men made a speech .... The condemned men mounted the scaffold, four coffins lay below. White hoods were pulled over their faces. The next moment four bodies shot into the air and continued to dangle there. Never have I forgotten the sight.

One of the earliest jails was in a stone house on Barrington Street, belonging at one time to Colonel Horseman of the Council. Later a jail was located on Hollis Street, but due either to the inefficiency of the jailer or the security system itself, large numbers of prisoners constantly escaped. In 1787 the jail was moved near the poorhouse on Spring Garden Road.

CITADEL

In the English fashion the jail was known as Bridewell.

When Halifax was incorporated in 1841 a red brick building (that had formerly served as a County Sessions building), used for a Merchants' Exchange and Reading Room, was taken over for City Hall. It was situated on the corner of George and Upper Water streets, very near the present Law Courts. By 1885 Mayor J.C. Mackintosh described it as "a disgrace to the city of Halifax .... a perfect pest hole, saturated with sewage, ill-ventilated, and unhealthy in the extreme."

Accordingly a most impressive new City Hall was constructed, its main en-

The occasionally rough-and-tumble life of a seaport town frequently required the cooperation of both civil and military authorities. If you stepped out of line in the mid-1870s, one or the other of these officers would want to talk about it with you! Courtesy, Halifax Police Department Museum

33

Halifax Police Officers are pictured on the Waterfront during the 1950s. In the postwar years, the city became a more settled place than in all of its past. Courtesy, Halifax Police Department Museum

trance at the north end of the Grand Parade, with a lower level entrance around the corner on Duke Street for the police station, courtroom, jail cells, and administrative offices. Although the police station now has a separate, modern building, City Hall still stands proudly Victorian in its historic location facing St. Paul's Church at the north end of the Grand Parade.

At one time there was a penitentiary on the shores of the Northwest Arm, abandoned in 1880 and demolished in 1948, when its stones were used in the construction of St. Mary's University. Prisoners were also housed in a jail behind the County Courthouse on Spring Garden Road, and grim Rockhead Prison stood at the north end of Gottingen Street until very recent times, when it made way for a modern housing development. Another forbidding but disused prison remains at Melville Island on property of the Armdale Yacht Club. Originally used for French and American prisoners of war, the cells now serve as lockers for members of the yacht club.

Before the regular police force was organized in 1864 there were twelve constables. Night watchmen in ordinary clothes, but distinguished by tall beaver hats and iron rattles, patrolled the streets

calling out the hours. The 1864 reorganization increased the number of constables to thirty, under six sergeants who were given their orders by the City Marshal or his deputy. Their territory was forbiddingly large—the entire peninsula, in days before the invention of automobiles or radios. Imagine the problem facing a lone policeman if he nabbed a drunk and disorderly person in the vicinity of the Northwest Arm and had to march him all the way down to the old Hollis Street jail!

The Halifax police had extra pressures during wartime, or with even the threat of war present. In 1776 special precautions were taken during the American Revolution when each night from sunset to sunrise two constables were augmented by the militia, which contributed an officer, a sergeant, a corporal, and ten privates to patrol the streets. Magistrates, too, took turns with all-night duty.

In wartime it has been the custom for military and naval patrols to assist local police. During the Second World War Royal Canadian Air Force security police were also included in the patrols. By 1944 the three services combined and patrolled the streets in speedy little jeeps.

When VE Day was declared high spirited groups of armed forces personnel and civilians became unruly gangs, causing a serious riot. Blame was laid at the door of the naval authorities by the Royal Commission, headed by Honorable Mr. Justice R.L. Kellock, who said, "In my opinion 156 Shore Patrol were quite insufficient numerically to deal with 9,500 ratings." His was a controversial decision even at the time, but today the scars have healed and Halifax citizens and the naval branch of the Canadian Armed Forces live together in harmony.

Times have changed since Governor Cornwallis laid the foundations of government and justice in Halifax. Government is democratic and justice is less harsh. One Halifax building has watched the transition serenely—St. Paul's Church. More will be learned about this church in the next chapter.

Above
Although the largest and best known, the VE Day Riot is only one of several disturbances pitting townsfolk against the military. Courtesy, Halifax Police Department Museum

Left
Rioting followed the end of hostilities in Europe. A mixture of relief and resentment sent military and civilian populations into the streets. Courtesy, Halifax Police Department Museum

IN HONOUR OF
THOSE WHO SERVED

IN MEMORY OF
THOSE WHO FELL

1914   1918
1939   1945

Although one of the city's foremost landmarks, St. Paul's Church was actually fabricated in New England and assembled on its location. First opened in 1750, the church retains an active congregation generations later. Photo by Dean Brousseau

end of the city and to Africville on the outskirts. A petition to the government in 1861 asked that a school be established to serve these children.

In 1780 an Act of the Legislature authorized a lottery for the purpose of raising 1,500 pounds to "erect a proper and convenient building in the town of Halifax for keeping a public school." The lottery took place the following year, but since only 750 pounds were realized, it was not until 1789 that the Grammar School began, not in a building of its own, but in the one at the corner of Sackville and Barrington streets where the Assembly had been holding its sessions. The headmasters were Anglican clergymen who sometimes taught and preached as well. The last of these men, Reverend Dr. Edwin Gilpin, was head of the school for forty-one years. For a few of these years the school was located on Birmingham Street, connected by a passageway to Dr. Gilpin's house on Spring Garden Road.

Finally in 1877 citizens demanded a high school for all boys in the city, and one was opened in temporary quarters at the Freemason's Hall while a search went on for a suitable property for a permanent school building. The result was the construction of the Halifax County Academy on the corner of Sackville and Brunswick streets in 1879. It was not until 1885 that girls were admitted to the Academy. The old building had a long record as an excellent high school for the entire county and fortunately survived the Halifax explosion of 1917 when classes were in session. The last graduating class left in 1942, and since then the building has been used for administrative educational purposes.

In January 1814 Captain Walter Bromley, a recently retired paymaster of the 23rd Fusiliers, opened his Royal Acadian School in the old Theatre Royal on Argyle Street. It served children of any denomination or colour, illiterate adults (in the evenings), and on Sundays, young overworked apprentices. By 1816 Bromley had 400 pupils. Because he had difficulty obtaining textbooks, Bromley bought a printing press on which he turned out his own texts.

In the early 1820s the old theatre was replaced by a new stone school which included living quarters for Bromley. He returned to England in 1828 and must have been sorely missed. The school continued until the early 1900s and, although it still stands today, the building has been used as a printing shop and for other purposes since the First World War.

In his reminiscences William Brown had this to say about the schools of his boyhood:

The cheapest price for a child at school was four dollars a year at the Royal Acadian School; the [Grammar] school was eight dollars a year and private school teachers received from three to five dollars a quarter for each pupil . . . .

Severe punishment was thought to be the best correction for evil. In our schools, boys were "hoisted" and birched, and at later time were severely beaten on the hand with a round ruler.

Further north on Argyle street a large

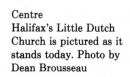

Centre
Halifax's Little Dutch Church is pictured as it stands today. Photo by Dean Brousseau

three-story wooden building was erected in 1818 by the Church of England and named the National School. There were 117 children attending it the first year. Later in the nineteenth century the building housed the Victoria School of Art and Design, which was promoted by Mrs. Anna Leonowens, remembered today as the heroine in the play *Anna and the King of Siam.* The building has since been converted to smart restaurants, overlooking the Grand Parade.

At first Catholic children attended Bromley's Royal Acadian School or the Grammar School, depending on the affluence of their parents. A provincial statute of 1766 stated that any Popish recusant who set up a school would be imprisoned for three months and fined ten pounds. The children were taught their Catechism at the church after regular school hours.

In 1802 Father Burke petitioned the Assembly for the right to set up a school and a seminary, but he was flatly refused. Anglican Bishop Inglis wrote that such seminaries would be "prolific hotbeds of Popery." Undaunted Father Burke had a large wooden building constructed next to his church and in 1806 he got the necessary government permission. By 1820 there were more than 100 boys in the school and a separate school had been arranged to accommodate 193 girls.

The school system developed at a more rapid pace when the Free School Act was passed in 1864. Until recently schools were rather loosely classified along religious lines. Within the last several decades the establishment of vocational schools in Halifax and Dartmouth, as well as the Nova Scotia Institute of Technology, have greatly enhanced possible career choices for students.

King's College (built in 1789 at Windsor), the first university in the Commonwealth to receive a Royal Charter, was a disappointment to the people of the province, who were soon disabused of the notion that it was open to all denominations. Even Bishop Charles Inglis was unable to dissuade Judge Alexander Croke (who was on the Board of Governors)

from making it a purely Anglican university, in spite of the fact that all citizens were paying for its upkeep through their taxes.

In 1820 the cornerstone of Dalhousie University was laid by the Lieutenant Governor, the Earl of Dalhousie, at the north end of the Grand Parade, and the school was "open to all classes and denominations." Because of political and religious wrangling it did not begin to flourish until the 1880s, when it rapidly outgrew its original building and moved to the Forrest Building on the present University Avenue. Dalhousie's faculties of Law and Medicine and its close ties with the Bedford Institute of Oceanography have established for it an international reputation for this, and it is the major university in Halifax.

In 1912 Dalhousie's campus enlarged to include the Studley estate, once the property of Judge Croke. King's College

Centre
The students of Dalhousie University (once located in downtown Halifax) retain the right to graze livestock on the grounds that are now occupied by City Hall. This 1860 photograph shows the University's first home, now the seat of municipal government. Courtesy, Dalhousie University

CHAPTER V

WELLS, LAMPS, AND TRAMS

For ninety-nine years Haligonians were supplied with drinking water from private and public wells. Pumps were located throughout the city and homeowners sent their children or servants to the nearest neighbourhood pump with two wooden buckets on a hoop to replenish the water supply throughout the day. Newspapers of 1847 reported no less than four well drownings—two female servants and two soldiers were the unlucky victims in four separate incidents. One, as reported in the July 24, 1847, *Acadian Recorder* portrayed an astonishing contrast to life in Halifax today:

The body of a soldier, belonging to the 89th Regiment, was discovered in the garrison well on the road to the Exercising Ground yesterday afternoon at two o'clock. Some persons who would have used the water within a few days, were prevented by its rancidity, and the mere taste of it was enough to sicken any person; but as the well was never much resorted to, except by washerwomen, or in times of great drought, none supposed on discovering the badness of the water of late that it was affected by any other than ordinary causes. On yesterday afternoon, however, a lad, in the employ of Mr. Palmer Inglis, happened to drop a bucket in the well, and having procured a hook, in grappling for the bucket brought up a soldier's forage cap with the number 89 in brass figures affixed to it. The corpse was then discovered, and has been recognized to be the body of a man, a favourite servant of Lieutenant Colonel Thorpe, of the 89th Regiment, who unaccountably disappeared about Christmas last.

Fortunately piped water was on its way into the city. The Halifax Water Company's Act of Incorporation had been passed on April 19, 1844, and the first water came into the city on September 29, 1848, from the Chain Lakes. While some householders and businesses were eager to have water installed, others were reluctant to pay for water that had always been free. The Water Company had a contract to supply the city with eighteen hydrants and twenty-five fire plugs for 400 pounds annually, and citizens made use of the hydrants in the same way they had used the old pumps. The Halifax Steam Boat Company welcomed the new arrangement eagerly, because up to that time sea water had been used in the ferries' boilers, causing dangerous salt accumulations.

In 1861 the city purchased the Halifax Water Company and set up a commission to run the water department. Gradually the old wells disappeared and all residents had water piped to their homes, but a great deal of trouble was caused by improper installations. Uninsulated pipes froze, burst, and water ran continually, lowering the pressure and turning sidewalks and streets into miniature glaciers. To prevent their pipes from bursting many people kept the water running slowly at all times in frigid weather—low-

ering the pressure to the point where residents in some areas got no water at all.

In 1944 the business of the city's water supply was taken over by the Public Service Commission, set up to deal with the kind of problems that were occuring all over North America. The population of the city was outgrowing the source of the water supply, ancient pipes were developing underground leaks, and pumping stations were becoming outdated. New developments had also taken place in regard to metering, chlorination, fluoridation, and the addition of lime to water that had a high acid content.

The Public Service Commission, financially independent of the City of Halifax, made plans for a major change in the water system to come into effect during the late 1970s. There was some danger of a water shortage before the new system became operational, so in cooperation with the City of Dartmouth a pipe carrying water from Dartmouth's Lake Major was brought across the Angus L. MacDonald Bridge. That threat of a water shortage passed with the opening of the new Pockwock system, which can supply thirty-two million gallons of water a day, twelve million more than now required. The Pockwock system, which incorporates all the latest technical advances, including computerized monitoring, cost fifty-one million dollars, but is projected to take care of the needs of Halifax for many years to come. In addition the Public Service Commission has recently purchased Tomahawk Lake for future expansion when the need arises.

The water supply of a city is of great importance to fire fighters, particularly so in a city of wooden buildings. The first fire regulations in Halifax were published in 1752, giving the magistrates the right to order a house to be pulled down or blown up to stop a fire from raging through a complete block. Governor Lawrence had wells dug and pumps installed specifically for fire fighting, and, like the other wells in the town, these were the responsibility of the magistrates. Firewards were appointed by the Justices of

Pictured is the official residence of the Public Gardens Superintendent. Photo by Dean Brousseau

forty-five hours and twenty minutes. The first plane carrying airmail from Ottawa to Halifax landed on Banook Lake in Dartmouth in 1928.

In the early 1930s Halifax Municipal Airport became a reality beside Chebucto Road, where Saunders Park and Westmount subdivision are located today. A stylized sculpture in the park is a memorial to Wing Commander Donald W. Saunders, manager of the airport and instructor of the Halifax Flying Club. Pan American Airways had a triweekly service from Halifax to Boston, carrying passengers and airmail. The fare was thirty-five dollars for the six-hour flight in twin-engined Sikorsky amphibian planes.

When World War II broke out the flying field was taken over for barracks, the Flying Club moved to Stanley airport in the valley, and commercial flights thereafter landed at Eastern Passage where the Royal Canadian Air Force (RCAF) had expanded Admiral Byrd's seaplane base to a land base as well. The first Trans Canada Air Lines plane (now Air Canada) that flew into Halifax landed at this airport on April 16, 1941. Maritime Central Airways (later Eastern Provincial, and now owned by Canadian Pacific) also began operations there in the early 1940s.

In 1948 the RCAF turned the Eastern Passage airport over to the Royal Canadian Navy (RCN), and the entire area was named Shearwater. Commercial airlines continued to use its facilities until the Halifax International Airport (near Enfield) was completed in September 1960. From the airport, buses and taxis whisk passengers in to Halifax or Dartmouth where, since 1981, buses of the Metropolitan Transit Commission serve both cities—a contrast to the days of sedan chairs.

The first mass transportation system in Halifax was William D. O'Brien's Halifax City Railroad, composed of five cars pulled by horses on tracks that extended from Richmond Station in the North to the end of Pleasant (now Barrington) Street in the South. It began operations in 1866,

but stopped ten years later when the ICR moved the main railway station from Richmond to North Street. O'Brien's tracks were torn up in the process.

From 1873 to 1895 another horse-drawn conveyance, Colonel B.H. Hornsby's omnibus, operated from the center of Halifax out to Willow Park in an east-west direction, but Haligonians travelling from North to South had to wait until 1886 before trams pulled by horses were again in operation—this time by the Halifax Street Railway Company. This American firm was bought by the Nova Scotia Power Company in 1890, which suffered a great loss by fire in 1895. A group of prominent Halifax businessmen bought the remains of the business and in 1896, as the Halifax Tramway Company, put the first electric trams into service. Routes were expanded, and in 1917 the Nova Scotia Tramway and Power Company took over.

Some Haligonians will remember with nostalgia the yellow Birney streetcars that were first used in 1920 and served until 1949. At that time the Nova Scotia Light and Power Company, which had been operating the system since 1939, changed to trolley coaches—buses powered by electricity from overhead wires. The old streetcar tracks were either torn up or buried under new pavement.

In 1970 Halifax Transit Corporation took over from Nova Scotia Light and Power and replaced the trolley coaches with silver and purple diesel buses that gave way in 1981 to the present white, blue, and silver fleet sporting the brilliant green logo of the Metropolitan Transit Commission and serving not only Halifax but the greater metropolitan area. Halifax has come a long way since the sea was its only highway.

In 1932 CBC set up an office in Halifax. CBC's more recent offices are pictured here. Photo by John R. Davis

Extending from the extreme north to the extreme south of the city, Barrington Street will probably always remain one of Halifax's busiest thoroughfares. This photograph from the 1880s is in marked contrast to the activity on the same intersection a century later. From the Photograph Collection of the Public Archives of Nova Scotia

CHAPTER VII

TRADE AND COMMERCE

The advertisement in the *London Gazette* of March 1749 that lured settlers to Halifax promised them free food for the passage and for twelve months after their arrival. A sample of items from the accounts found in Dr. T.B. Akins' *History of Halifax City* show these government expenditures:

Blankets, woolens, and shoes for settlers, and presents for Indians—1,325 pounds. Cash paid for victualling settlers—12,068 pounds. Treasurer of the Navy's account for bedding and victualling during voyage—7,354 pounds.

Merchants of New England did a thriving business, such as Apthorp & Hancock of Boston who were paid almost 7,000 pounds for "materials, vessels and stores." One merchant, Malachi Salter, already familiar with Chebucto having been in the harbour in 1744 in connection with the fishery, later became a prominent Halifax citizen. Salter Street is named after him.

Two men who held positions of trust in Cornwallis' government were suspected of unscrupulous dealings during those early years. One, Otis Little, the first Attorney General and Commissary of Stores, was dismissed after settlers of Dartmouth reported shortages in their provisions. The other, Joshua Mauger, victualler to the navy, first in Louisbourg and then in Halifax, was thought by Governor Cornwallis to be carrying on illicit trade with Louisbourg, but concrete evidence could not be found.

Mauger had a distillery near the Dockyard and owned a large fleet of ships, including privateers. He was one of the first merchants to trade with the West Indies (fish and lumber for rum, molasses, and sugar), and according to the following advertisement in the *Halifax Gazette* he also dealt in slaves:

In its role as a port city, Halifax readily made the transition from sail to steam. This photograph from the period immediately prior to World War I depicts the coaling of HMS *Ariadne.* From the Photograph Collection of the Public Archives of Nova Scotia

Just imported, and to be sold by Joshua Mauger at Major Lockman's store in Halifax, several Negro slaves as follows: a woman aged thirty-five, two boys aged twelve and thirteen respectively, two of eighteen, and a man aged thirty.

Mauger owned large tracts of property, including the beach on McNab's Island that still keeps his name—pronounced locally "Major's Beach." Mauger went to England and became Nova Scotia's first Agent General in 1761, never returning to Halifax.

Because the settlement of Halifax had been proposed by the Board of Trade and Plantations in 1748, it is fitting that one of the first organizations of 1750 in Halifax was an "Association for the Benefit of Trade." Its members were the merchants of the town. Under various names such as the Halifax Committee of

Trade, the Nova Scotia Commercial Society, the Society for Encouragement of Trade and Manufactures, to the present Halifax Board of Trade, merchants and businessmen have continually been at the very heart of progress and development in Halifax. This was the group that pressed for a Representative Government in 1758, who formed early marine and fire insurance companies, and who promoted trade with the Thirteen Colonies and the British West Indies.

Holding meetings at the Golden Ball, the Pontac Hotel, or the Merchants' Exchange, these men instituted the first banks, realized the possibilities of the Shubenacadie Canal, and saw the advantages of steam for navigation. They studied the market for Nova Scotia's natural resources—coal, gypsum, lumber, fish, and agricultural produce—and encouraged the formation of agricultural societies and the Mechanics Institute of 1832.

Names of Halifax businessmen appear in many facets of community life—as fire fighters; militiamen; assemblymen; councilmen; and shareholders in the Shubenacadie Canal Company, the Halifax Steam Boat Company, and the Poor Man's Friend Society. The same names occur over and over again.

During the first ten years in Halifax the business of supplying provisions for the fleets and military units that gathered here made for a very lively economy. Distilleries and breweries flourished and taxes on imported liquor were substantial sources of revenue. Merchants like Joshua Mauger, Michael Francklin, and Malachi Salter outfitted privateers and benefitted from the sale of prize ships.

Between the Seven Years' War (1756 to 1763) and the American Revolution (1776) a start was made to encourage civilian enterprises such as fishing, lumbering, and farming and to promote trade with the West Indies. The upheaval caused by the use of ships for lucrative privateering, the gravitation of able-bodied men to the army and navy, and the sudden influx of Loyalists slowed these endeavours. The lull just before the Napoleonic wars (1793 to 1814) saw another attempt to promote primary industry, and one of the most visible results was Lawrence Hartshorne and Jonathan Tremain's flour mill on the Dartmouth shore, built to insure a sufficient supply of that basic commodity.

Loyalists settled farms in Lawrencetown, Cole Harbour, and Preston and brought their produce to the Halifax market on the two ferry routes operated profitably by James Creighton and John Skerry. Inspired by John Young's "Agricola" letters published in Anthony Holland's newspaper, *The Acadian Recorder,* agriculture got a tremendous boost in 1818. At the same time the Lieutenant Governor, Lord Dalhousie, became president of the Agricultural Society and did much to encourage better farming throughout the province.

The War of 1812 again saw frantic ac-

tivity in the harbour with the economy stimulated by privateering and the sale of prize ships and their cargoes. Stirring events such as the capture of the U.S. frigate *Chesapeake* by the smaller HMS *Shannon* provided added excitement, and the arrival of black refugees, who had been former slaves of the Potomac and Chesapeake area, created new challenges for housing and provisions. Two previous waves of black immigrants, the slaves and servants who had accompanied their Loyalist masters and then the Maroons from Jamaica, had left in large numbers for Sierra Leone at the invitation of the British government. Those who came as a result of the War of 1812 settled in the same areas, and their descendants make up the largest part of the black population today. A depression followed the end of the war and by 1818 a soup kitchen administered by Samuel Cunard and Michael Tobin served 500 needy people a day.

On the other hand some citizens were wealthier than they had ever been. Dr. D.C. Harvey, Nova Scotia Archivist from 1931 until his retirement in 1956, wrote: "Between 1777 and 1814, nearly 800

In a desperate one-on-one engagement off the American coast in the summer of 1814, HMS *Shannon* helped reverse British fortunes at sea. Here the captured *Chesapeake* is seen being escorted into Halifax Harbour. From the Photograph Collection of the Public Archives of Nova Scotia

Illustrated is a typical streetscape of Halifax during the late nineteenth century. During this period the waterfront was lined with independent shipping, fishing, and chandlery companies. Etching by Donald Cameron Mackay. From the Collection of the Art Gallery of Nova Scotia

prizes were brought into Halifax harbour by privateers and ships of the navy . . . . This town was agog with the sale of prizes in the Vice-Admiralty Court and the profits that were made for all, officials and civilians."

Wealth generated the need for a bank. In 1801 and 1811 proposals were put forth to establish one, but both proposals came to nothing. It was then that Enos Collins, said to be the richest man in British North America as a result of his privateering activities, began his own private banking business in the ironstone building that today forms part of Halifax's Historic Properties on Upper Water Street.

Across the harbour in Dartmouth, north ferry operator John Skerry performed much the same service for resi-

dents of that village on a smaller scale.

Finally in 1825 the first official bank was opened in Collins' building and was called the Halifax Banking Company. Henry H. Cogswell was President, and Collins and Cunard were the main shareholders—the three *C*s. Others involved were William Pryor, James Tobin, John Clark, Joseph Allison, and Martin Gay Black. An advertisement in the *Acadian Recorder* gives the hours of business as being from ten to three o'clock—the same as for many banks today. Eventually this bank became the Canadian Imperial Bank of Commerce.

The Bank of Nova Scotia had its origins seven years later in 1832 at the corner of Duke and Granville streets. William Lawson was its first President. In 1864, not far away on Bedford Row, seven men formed the Merchants' Bank under a Federal Charter. In 1901 this became the Royal Bank of Canada, its head office moving to Montreal in 1907.

The standard currency of these early banks was not British sterling as might be expected, but rather the Spanish milled dollar, known in Boston, New York, and Toronto as "Halifax Currency" and worth five shillings. Even British troops were paid in Spanish silver because it was plentiful in the Western hemisphere, due in part to trade with the West Indies and Spanish colonies, as well as because Spanish dollars were minted in Mexico, Bolivia, Lima, Guatemala, San Diego, Santa Fe, and Spain itself. Halifax merchants had petitioned the military authorities as early as 1759 to proclaim it as the medium of exchange.

A petition to the Governor that gave the rate of exchange set by the merchants of 1811 was a confusing list of coins—guineas, Johannes, doubloons, eagles, and English and French crowns. On the whole, however, coins of any kind were scarce, and in 1817 private merchants issued their own tokens valued at a penny or half penny. These soon became too plentiful and were declared illegal. The following year an act was passed to issue paper money in denominations of

CHAPTER VIII

THE FINER ARTS

It is a simple matter of fact that Nova Scotia was the first of all the Provinces in the Dominion of Canada to cultivate literature. When Ontario was an unnamed wilderness and Quebec was without a printing press, Nova Scotia had its own newspapers and had begun to print its own books.

These words were written by the late Dr. Archibald MacMechan, Professor of English at Dalhousie University from 1889 to 1931. Halifax's first newspaper, the *Halifax Gazette*, appeared in 1752, and the first book was published in 1756. The latter was not exactly entertaining reading. It was a volume of Provincial laws, compiled by John Duport, Esquire. Dr. Cochran, a Loyalist from New York who was later principal of King's College, Windsor, produced the first literary magazine in the province in 1789—*The Nova Scotia Magazine and Comprehensive Review of Literature, Politics, and News.*

Like several of its successors Cochran's *Review* was short-lived. *The Novator* followed it in 1809, *The Acadian Magazine* in 1826, *The Halifax Monthly Magazine* in 1830, then *The Pearl, The Mayflower,* and *The Provincial* in quick succession. The last two were edited by women, who were also poets—Mary Eliza Herbert and Mary Jane Katzmann. *The Provincial* won high praise from subscribers in other parts of Canada and the United States. Its editor, Mrs. William Lawson, won the Akins Historical Prize in 1887 for her book *History of the Townships of Dartmouth, Preston, and Lawrencetown.*

The first book of general interest was printed in Halifax by Joseph Howe and published in 1829. It was Thomas Chandler Haliburton's *An Historical and Statistical Account of Nova Scotia,* released in two volumes. Haliburton was a prolific author, best remembered today for his tales of Sam Slick, the Yankee clockmaker.

Dartmouth poet Andrew Shiels' narrative poem, *The Witch of the Westcot*, was pub-

79

Anthony Henry, a fifer of the Royal Americans, arrived in Halifax in 1758 and, as most soldiers were allowed to supplement their pay by working in town, he went to work at Bushell's printing press. Later he secured a discharge from the army and within two years became manager of the *Halifax Gazette,* the first newspaper in Canada. Anthony Henry is buried with his wife in St. Paul's cemetery. Photo by John C. Davie

lished in 1831, also by Joseph Howe, who at that time was taking an interest in poetry, his own and that of others. From about 1830 on, books written on a wide range of subjects began to appear in Halifax. In 1840 Edward Belcher wrote an account of *H.M.S. Sulphur's Voyage Around the World, 1836-1843.* Sir John William Dawson, first Superintendent of Education in Nova Scotia, later Principal of McGill, was the author of over a dozen educational and scientific books. Dr. Abraham Gesner, discoverer of kerosene, published his first book in 1836, *Remarks on the Geology and Mineralogy of Nova Scotia.* Reverend George Munro Grant, minister of St. Matthew's Church in Halifax, journeyed across Canada in 1872 with Sir Sanford Fleming and published *Ocean to Ocean* the following year—the first cross-Canada travel book. Miss Marshall Saunders wrote over two dozen children's books, and her *Beautiful Joe,* published in 1893, sold well over 500,000 copies.

Halifax has produced an extraordinary number of authors who have been inspired by Nova Scotia's colourful history. Beamish Murdoch's three volume *History of Nova Scotia* and his cousin Thomas Akins' *History of Halifax City* were early examples. There have been several biographies of the well-known Joseph Howe, among them two recent ones by Kay Hill (for young people) and by Dr. J. Murray Beck. There are also Dr. Archibald Mac-Mechan's *Sagas of the Sea* and *Old Province Tales;* Dr. Hugh MacLennan's *Barometer Rising;* Colonel William Coates Borrett's *Tales Told Under the Old Town Clock;* Dr. Helen Creighton's collections of Nova Scotia folk songs and folk tales; Kay Hill's Micmac legends for children; Dr. Phyllis Blakeley's *Glimpses of Halifax, 1867-1900;* Thomas Raddall's *Halifax, Warden of the North;* Dr. John Martin's *The Story of Dartmouth;* Elsie Tolson's *The Captain, the Colonel, and Me* (stories of the Bedford-Sackville area); and Dr. Brian Cuthbertson's biography of Sir John Wentworth.

One explanation of the proliferation of

writers in the Halifax area is the availability of material for research. There has been a library in Halifax since 1832, and today's facilities for reading and research comprise perhaps a dozen libraries (including university facilities), the Public Archives of Nova Scotia, and several museums. The Nova Scotia Poetry Society and the Nova Scotia Branch of the Canadian Author's Association have helped encourage local writers for several years, and in 1975 the Writers' Federation of Nova Scotia (WFNS) was founded, giving further guidance to would-be authors through general meetings and panel discussions, publication of *Writers' News*, a manuscript reading service, annual contests, professional advice, and a generally supportive atmosphere. As one of the eight members of the Cultural Federations of Nova Scotia, WFNS receives financial assistance from the Department of Culture, Recreation, and Fitness.

Publishing has also undergone extensive changes in recent years, and with the help of the Canada Council, the Atlantic

Robert Wilkie's circa 1860 oil painting of *Halifax Harbour from Windmill Pier Dartmouth* clearly illustrates the town's continuing military role in the affairs of the British Empire. The most prominent details in this illustration draw attention to fortifications on George's Island, the Citadel, and visiting ships of the Royal Navy. From the Collection of the Art Gallery of Nova Scotia

Above
Halifax Harbour and
Bedford Basin were well
known as meeting places
long before the arrival of
Europeans. For hundreds
of years the Micmacs of
the South Shore held
gatherings in the area at
the close of every sum-
mer. The family group
shown in Robert Petley's
watercolour dates from
the 1840s. From the Col-
lection of the Art Gallery
of Nova Scotia

Right
This view of Halifax was
dedicated to His Excel-
lency Sir Gaspard Le
Marchant, Lieutenant
Governor of Nova Scotia,
by the publishers Smith
Bros. & Co. Courtesy,
New York Public Library

Left
On June 21, 1749, Governor Edward Cornwallis and some 2,500 others first established the foundations of Halifax. Though much has changed, the city still owes much of its character to its original purpose as a strategic stronghold. From the Photograph Collection of the Public Archives of Nova Scotia

Below
Contrary to popular assumption the name of the city was not borrowed from Halifax, England, but from George Dunk, second Earl of Halifax. During the time of the town's establishment Dunk was President of the Board of Trade and was responsible for the administration of the colonies. Governor Cornwallis named the new town in his honour. From the Collection of the Art Gallery of Nova Scotia

Above
During the nineteenth century the Halifax-Dartmouth area was a major centre for all sorts of small-craft racing. J.W. Gray's engraving of *The Four-Oared International Boat-Race* from 1871 gives some impression of the mass appeal such events could generate. From the Collection of the Art Gallery of Nova Scotia

Facing page, bottom
His Royal Highness Prince Edward, Duke of Kent, was Commander-in-Chief in Halifax. While there he ordered a garrison clock to be placed on the town side of Citadel Hill. Edward departed before the clock arrived from London in 1803. The Old Town Clock was installed in 1803 and remains as perhaps the best known feature of Halifax. Courtesy, Dartmouth Heritage Museum

Above
Although never a major feature of the city in the past, Halifax has in recent years become reliant on its growing number of restaurants. Haligonians have gained substantially from the competition between restauranteurs. Photo by John R. Davis

Right
In recent years Haligonians have come to enjoy a walk in the downtown area. One can never be too sure what a pedestrian will encounter, as street performers and promoters bid for the public's attention. These Spring Garden Road Bumble Bees are a fine example of how nature and humanity can coexist in harmony. Photo by John R. Davis

Above
In late July of every year local enthusiasts take part in the Halifax Natal Day Road Race. As this photograph clearly shows, the event has no lack of support and is witnessed by thousands during the early part of the founding-day celebrations. Photo by John R. Davis

Throughout its history as a major naval base, no foreign power has ever attempted a raid on Halifax. Pictured are the guns of York Redoubt, as they might have appeared in the 1890s. This installation is but one of many used to protect the city from the eighteenth century until the close of World War II. Photo by John R. Davis

Above
Built in 1803 at the instruction of the Duke of Kent, the Old Garrison Clock has marked the time through the city's many military involvements. Now known as "The Old Town Clock," it remains as the most well remembered of the city's many landmarks. Photo by John R. Davis

Left
At the corner of Brunswick and Gerrish streets is the building well known as "The Little Dutch Church." In the 1750s a group of some 2,250 mainly German-speaking settlers (Deutsch) established themselves and completed this structure by 1760. Photo by John R. Davis

Above
In over 200 years the centre of activity on Halifax Harbour has never varied. The contemporary skyline of the downtown now covers the area originally enclosed by palisades in 1749, and the surrounding city extends for several miles around this pivotal spot. Photo by John R. Davis

Facing page, top
The Fortress at Louisbourg is viewed across Louisbourg Harbour. Courtesy, The Image Farm

Right
The great stone tower in Fleming Park dominates the vistas along the North West Arm. The Memorial

Tower, as it is known, was built in commemoration
of the 150th anniversary of the birth of representa-
tional government in the British Empire. Its patron,
Sir Sanford Fleming, was of the opinion that elected assemblies within the Empire all followed as a
consequence of the constitutional events in Nova
Scotia. Photo by John R. Davis

This photograph of machine-shop workers from the 1890s illustrates a continuing tradition of expertise in maintaining naval readiness. The original facility established for the Royal Navy is now kept by the Canadian armed forces. From the Photograph Collection of the Public Archives of Nova Scotia

Ordnance Yard during
the late nineteenth
century became a scene of
diminished activity as the
concerns of the Empire
shifted to other parts of
the globe. Etching by
Donald Cameron Mac-
Kay. From the Collection
of the Art Gallery of
Nova Scotia

The Halifax Academy Cadet Corps' "A" Company is pictured at attention in 1913. Courtesy, James W. Creighton

assist the army.

Wartime tensions mounted in Halifax once more during the American Civil War of 1861 to 1865. All defenses were strengthened, a powder magazine was constructed below Wellington Barracks just off north Barrington Street, and at Ives Point on McNab's Island a new battery appeared. Such activities created employment and a boom in the economy. Merchants prospered not only because of these local enterprises, but because of brisk trade with the Confederates. Many Halifax youths, including one of Joe Howe's sons, joined the Northern Union army, lured by the good pay, but generally Haligonians favoured the Southerners. In 1864 the *Tallahassee,* a Confederate cruiser responsible for sinking many Union ships, fled into Halifax Harbour while being pursued by two enemy ships. Thinking they had the *Tallahassee* trapped, the ships waited just outside the harbour. After refuelling, however, local pilot Jock Fleming guided the big steamship out through the eastern passage of the harbour on a high tide in the dead of night, thus neatly evading her pursuers. The *Tallahassee's* Captain, John Taylor Wood, retired to Halifax at the end of the war and was much in demand as a speaker to tell of this and his other wartime adventures.

A quiet, depressed interval of peace followed, until the Boer War broke out in 1899, and British regiments throughout the Empire headed for South Africa. The Royal Canadian Regiment replaced the Imperial troops at the Citadel. By early 1900 many of their number, including the "H" Company of Halifax, left for South Africa from the deepwater terminals near the Dockyard after a training period in the newly constructed red sandstone armouries. Sailing on the troopships *Laurentian, Koomeranian,* and *Milwaukee,* no longer redcoats but clad in khaki, Canadians were soon involved in the fighting at Witpoort, Mafeking, and Paardeberg.

By year's end they were back. The *Bluenose,* a short-lived Halifax periodical, recommended a fitting memorial:

Let it be the man in 'khaki'. . . . the typical Canadian as he looked with his rifle in his hands and his face stern and determined, just as the real Canadians in khaki appeared the day they went to Paardeberg.

On the grounds of Province House a larger-than-life soldier now stands atop the memorial, decorated with scenes of the war in bas-relief and unveiled by the Duke and Duchess of Cornwall and York, who later became King George V and Queen Mary.

The Imperial troops were back, too, but not for long. In 1906 the British Government turned the defense of the country over to the Canadian government. Halifax seemed suddenly devoid of colour and activity when the last British soldiers sailed for England, and ships of the Royal Navy left the harbour. The Citadel, the Dockyard, the forts, and the batteries on the outskirts fell asleep, except for a few soldiers who were little more than caretakers. In the summertime militia units enlivened the scene to a certain extent, and a small Royal Canadian Naval College was set up in the Dockyard. Yet the pomp and ceremony, the spit and polish of the old days, had vanished from Halifax. Social life had slowed to a crawl, merchants missed the officers' trade, sportsmen missed the competition of teams from the garrison and the fleet, and the entire populace missed the colour of uniformed men in the streets and band music on summer nights in the Public Gardens.

When war was declared in August 1914 Halifax was far from prepared, but before long there were volunteer regiments manning outpost stations like York Redoubt and McNab's Island. Small vessels were pressed into mine-sweeping service and anti-submarine nets were stretched across the eastern passage and from either side of George's Island. At Pier Two camouflaged liners like the *Mauretania* and *Olympic* transported almost all of the

For many Canadians the last image of Canada was observed from the deck of a troop ship leaving Halifax Harbour. Over 60,000 Canadians perished during the Great War. Etching by Arthur Lismer. From the Collection of the Art Gallery of Nova Scotia

Canadian contingents going overseas. Rumours of spies within the city and submarines just off the coast circulated and helped to distract customers who grumbled about sharply rising prices. Convoys assembled in Bedford Basin and once again Royal Navy warships made Halifax a regular port of call.

Returning troop ships brought casualties back from the front, and those destined for Halifax were subjected to crowded quarters in hospitals there until Camp Hill Military Hospital, built on the site used long ago for troops under canvas, opened its doors in 1917. Prisoners of war were also brought to Halifax. Some were kept in the Citadel, and some were put in the stone prison on Melville Island.

Prohibition came to Nova Scotia in 1916, but bootleggers, prostitutes, and the increased wartime population made life difficult for local police. Service clubs and churches tried to make life easier for

the troops stationed in the area, and other groups organized bazaars and entertainments to raise money for the Canadian Patriotic Fund and the Belgian Relief Fund.

When the United States entered the war in 1917 vessels from the United States Navy were in and out of the harbour. By 1918 the American seaplane base had been established at Eastern Passage for reconnaissance work, with about 200 personnel.

Due to wartime activities Halifax must have suffered more disruption than any other city in Canada, and certainly needed no further problems. Suddenly, however, on the clear, sunny morning of December 6, 1917, came a disaster that seemed for a time to be an insurmountable catastrophe. Two ships, steaming toward each other, zigzagged like two people on a sidewalk who step from side to side to avoid each other, but seem drawn together as if by invisible magnets. As the Belgian Relief vessel *Imo* was coming out of Bedford Basin it collided with the *Mont Blanc,* a French ship flying the red flag that signified it was carrying explosives (TNT, picric acid, and benzine). The two ships collided in the Narrows and the drums of benzine on the deck of the *Mont Blanc* burst into flames. Not realizing the danger of the situation, boats from the shore, in addition to the new Halifax fire truck, rushed to the scene to help. People crowded vantage points around the harbour to watch the blaze. At 9:05 a.m., seventeen minutes after the collision, there was a mighty roar and blast as the *Mont Blanc* exploded in the worst man-made explosion in history until the Hiroshima disaster.

The bedrock of Halifax trembled as in an earthquake. Buildings collapsed, trapping their occupants. Shards of red-hot metal, spears of window glass, and falling beams caused death, destruction, and injuries throughout Halifax, Dartmouth, and Bedford. Stoves were overturned, starting fires in houses already devasted. A tidal wave lashed the shores, swamping boats and drowning people who had sur-

CHAPTER XI

NOTABLE VISITORS TO HALIFAX

Halifax, because of its naval and military importance, has had more members of the Royal Family as visitors than any other city in Canada. As a result Haligonians are ardent Royalists. School children in every generation have been marched to the slopes of the Citadel, the Commons, or to the foot of Fort Needham hoping to glimpse royal visitors while welcoming them with three hearty cheers and singing "Will Ye No Come Back Again?" Crowds line the streets on which royal carriages or limousines are expected to pass en route to Government House or Province House. Almost every citizen has at one time or another participated in a massed choir, pageant, parade, or sports event to welcome royal guests. Homes, business establishments, and streets are decorated with flags and bunting, while protocol officers worry over guest lists for luncheons, dinners, and balls.

Other distinquished visitors, especially in earlier times, seem not to have experienced such a warm welcome. John James Audubon, the famous American naturalist, approached Halifax by stagecoach in 1833 en route home from Pictou where he had been visiting Thomas MacCulloch. The stagecoach waited for an hour on the Dartmouth side before crossing the harbour, while the crew of the ferry boat finished breakfast. Audubon wrote:

We crossed the harbour in which we saw a sixty-four gun flagship riding at anchor. The coach drove up to the house of Mr. Paul, the best hotel, where we with difficulty obtained one room with four beds for six persons. With a population of eighteen thousand souls, and two thousand more of soldiers, Halifax has not one good hotel, and only two very indifferent private boarding houses where the attendance is miserable and the table by no means good. We are, however, settled . . . .

The Nova Scotia New Monthly Magazine of February 1842 reported on another notable visitor, Charles Dickens:

On the 20th of January Mr. Dickens arrived in Halifax on the steamer Britannia. *We had expected that the literati of the Metropolis would have proposed some plan whereby the inhabitants might welcome so worthy a guest, but no such manifestation appeared.*

Dickens visited Province House and afterward wrote his impressions in *American Notes:*

It was like looking at Westminster through the wrong end of the telescope. The Governor delivered the speech from the Throne. The military band outside struck up "God Save the Queen" with great vigour; the people shouted; the Ins rubbed their hands; the Outs shook their heads; the Government party said there never was such a good speech; the Opposition declared there never was such a bad one; and in short everything went on and promised to go on just as it does at home.

Almost one hundred years later at the height of the Second World War, news flew around the city that a merchant ship (a great trooper) had arrived in the harbour bearing another very famous Englishman. This was Winston Churchill, en route to Quebec in August 1943 to the first Quebec Conference with President Roosevelt. Churchill was accompanied by his wife, and daughter, Mary, and a subaltern in an anti-aircraft battery, who was acting as his aide-de-camp. They had crossed the Atlantic in the *Queen Mary.* Although the visit was supposed to be top secret, word got out and crowds gathered near the train that was taking them to Quebec. Complete with cigar and giving a "V for Victory" sign, Churchill talked informally to his fans, and led them in a singsong of "O Canada" and "The Maple Leaf."

After the Quebec Conference, the Churchills reappeared in Halifax for the return voyage on the battleship *Renown.*

Just before boarding, Churchill had a sudden desire to see some of the city. Rear Admiral Leonard Murray drove him around (the rest of the party following in another car) and then stopped at the Citadel, the Public Gardens, and Point Pleasant Park. There were many startled people in these places who instantly recognized Churchill and went home to tell their doubting families of their encounter. Because of wartime secrecy, it was not publicized until well after the event. When he was finally on board the *Renown* and saying his farewells, Churchill observed, "Now we know Halifax is not only a shed on the wharf as we had known it to be before."

The following September, Churchill came again to Halifax on the *Queen Mary* for the second Quebec Conference, but this time he managed to get on board his train and away with no publicity. Thirty-six years later, in 1980, Halifax Mayor Edmund Morris unveiled Oscar Nemon's larger-than-life statue of Churchill, which stands in front of the Halifax Memorial Library. It is a constant reminder of the admiration Haligonians felt for this giant of a man throughout the days of the Second World War.

An unusual visitor who came to Halifax in September 1984 during his Canadian tour was Pope John Paul II. The pope landed at Shearwater Airport, where he was welcomed by Roman Catholic dignitaries and government representatives. Travelling in one of the two "popemobiles" especially designed for his Canadian tour, he waved and smiled at the hundreds of cheering spectators who lines the route through Eastern Passage, Dartmouth, and Halifax where he stopped at the North Common to attend an "Accent on Youth" rally.

At the Common an enormous four-tiered altar had been constructed, each tier banked with potted evergreens—4,500 in all. Behind the altar were seven nautical-looking masts representing the seven sacraments, dominated by a large cross. Young people assembled in the quadrants divided by fencing, heard the

grumble about the expense to the country of maintaining the monarchy should inquire about the salaries that would have to be paid to public relations persons who might attempt such a task, if they even could. The thread of continuity woven as each succeeding generation of the Royal Family visits Commonwealth countries, their presence evoking a sense of the return of close relatives, could never be accomplished by any paid diplomats.

On their way to the Olympics at Montreal in 1976 the Queen and Prince Philip arrived in Halifax on July 13 aboard the *Britannia* from Boston, having attended United States Bicentennial Celebrations. They were greeted by Honorable Allan MacEachen. After a Royal Salute at the Dockyard and inspection of the Guard of Honour, they met the Provincial Cabinet members, then went to City Hall and turned the sod for the nearby Metro Centre. A new departure was a reception on *Britannia* for members of the media, after which came lunch at Government House with Lieutenant Governor and Mrs. Clarence L. Gosse.

At the Halifax shipyards the royal couple inspected an oil-drilling rig and an

oil-drilling ship, both under construction, and visited senior citizens at Northwood Center. Prince Philip presented Duke of Edinburgh medals to the outstanding young people who had won them, and the Queen presented the Prince of Wales Yacht racing cup to its winner. All of these awards were made on the *Britannia.* A private dinner on the Royal Yacht followed, and the day ended with a reception.

July 14 included a visit to Dartmouth City Hall where members of City Council and others were presented, then on to Shearwater, from where they flew to Greenwood, drove to Windsor and Wolfville, and came back for the government dinner at the Hotel Nova Scotian (renamed in the bilingual fashion of the day). The next day, Thursday, July 15, the Queen and Prince Philip flew to Fredericton and then continued on to the Olympics.

History in Halifax, with regard to royalty, repeats itself, and the present Prince of Wales, Prince Charles, paid an unofficial visit to Halifax on *Minerva,* in August 1973 when he was a sublieutenant. Ten years later he was back with his beautiful wife, Princess Diana, and a new

Kris Kristofferson and Anne Murray, a Nova Scotia-born singer, filmed a Christmas special in Halifax in 1982. Courtesy, Precision Photographic Services

generation of enthusiastic monarchists was born. The young couple arrived at CFB Shearwater, and were greeted by Honorable Allan J. MacEachen, Deputy Prime Minister, and Governor General and Mrs. Edward Schreyer. Once again cheering crowds thronged their route as they drove across the bridge to the Garrison Grounds for the customary inspection of the Guard of Honour and the Royal Salute. The lovely Diana's costumes were much admired, but the warmth of her personality and her interest in meeting the crowds who surrounded her on informal walk-abouts was a most remarkable quality in one so young.

Seemingly tireless and always cheerful, both Prince Charles and Princess Diana talked to old and young, shook hands endlessly, and never lost their patience when pushed to the point where most people would probably have had a severe case of claustrophobia. Following the pattern of the Queen and Duke of Edinburgh's last visit, they entertained the media at a reception on the *Britannia,* followed by another reception for invited guests who viewed the "Beat the Retreat" ceremony by the Royal Marine Band.

The following day the Prince and Princess of Wales went to the Dockyard, where they unveiled a plaque commemorating their visit, saw the huge new ship-repair unit, and then traveled to St. George's Church, which had been built at the request of Prince Charles' great-great-great-grandfather, the Duke of Kent. There they unveiled another plaque, and went on by jeep to the North Common, where 8,000 people were waiting in a miserable drizzle to greet them. School choirs and a ukulele group of 2,000 children under the direction of Chalmers Doane, Supervisor of Music in Halifax Schools, performed, while hundreds of balloons were released into the mist. The Prince and Princess did another walk-about and planted trees on the Common while children surrounded them and presented them with gifts, including everything from wilted wild flowers to teddy bears and patchwork quilts for their baby son William.

That evening the state dinner was held at the Nova Scotian Hotel (which reverted to its original name under new ownership), and the Prince and Princess of Wales sat at the head table with Prime Minister Pierre Trudeau and Lieutenant Governor and Mrs. John Shaffner. Princess Diana was resplendent in a long, cream-coloured gown, a pearl and diamond tiara sparkling on her blond hair—a fairy tale princess with her handsome prince. The Prime Minister welcomed them to Canada, adding that the Atlantic Provinces were "the most friendly part of Canada."

After the dinner the young couple boarded the *Britannia,* and sailed that night to Shelburne for Loyalist Bicentennial celebrations. The band of the Royal Marines played "Auld Lang Syne" as the *Britannia* pulled away, escorted by HMCS *Assiniboine.* Another royal visit had ended for Halifax, but its citizens would watch the remainder of the Canadian tour on television with a somewhat proprietary air, having been the *first* to greet the Prince and Princess of Wales.

As succeeding generations of the Royal Family come to Halifax, a widespread air of excitement prevails. Plans are made for the familiar rituals, such as the greeting by dignitaries, a royal salute, a regimental inspection, parades through the streets, state dinners, and gala performances. Each generation of Haligonians rises to the occasion, showing the old landmarks to the royal visitors, in much the same way they would display the family album to a distant cousin. If by studying history we may gain insight into the future, young Prince William and Prince Henry, sons of the present Prince and Princess of Wales, should be stepping ashore at the Dockyard in about twenty years' time as midshipmen in the Royal Navy. When they do they will certainly be given a truly royal welcome in this historic city, founded during the reign of their ancestor, King George II, and steeped in British tradition.

Left
Prince Andrew was a royal visitor to the city in 1985. Courtesy, Precision Photographic Services

Above
Prince Charles and Princess Diana were caught by the camera during their visit to Halifax in July 1983. Courtesy, Precision Photographic Services

The tranquility of a Sunday in the Public Gardens was enjoyed by several in this photograph from 1975. Photo by John R. Davis

mouth, and Springhill areas. Meanwhile, the provincial power commission built generating plants in other parts of Nova Scotia for industries, smaller power utilities, and rural areas.

During World War II NSLP added more equipment to cope with the demands of wartime Halifax. Working with the Allies, the company discovered how to use electricity to protect ships from dangerous magnetic mines. About 1,600 war and merchant ships, including the *Queen Elizabeth,* were demagnetized in Halifax Harbour by NSLP. Fear arose that the firm's generating and tramway headquarters on Water Street would be a target for German commandos. The area was fortified with sandbags and barbed wire, but no attack came.

Demand for electricity climbed after the war. From 1946 to 1956 power generation in the province increased 150 percent as both NSLP and the power commission acquired old generating stations or built new ones. NSLP also modernized its Halifax tram service in 1949 and the city became the first in North America with a fleet of electric trolley buses. NSLP would supplement these with diesel-powered buses in 1963, before selling the system to the city in 1969.

To better supply power customers, all generating plants of NSLP and the Nova Scotia Power Commission were linked in 1962. By then most rivers were already tapped for hydro power, so further electricity came from more expensive coal- or oil-powered stations. Although both utilities were studying ways of harnessing the tides in the Bay of Fundy, the idea was still unworkable. During the 1960s, with provincial electricity requirements still growing, the two companies were each generating about the same amount of power for customers. Metro Halifax was the province's largest power market, and to meet its demand NSLP opened the $18-million Tufts Cove

generating station in 1965. The Dartmouth facility was the biggest of its kind in Eastern Canada, but in just four years NSLP began doubling the new plant's generating capacity to keep up with metro's needs.

In late 1971 the provincial government announced that the Nova Scotia Power Commission would take over NSLP, the second-largest private utility in Canada, and consolidate all power operations. Shock and surprise followed, but the "provincialization" of the power system was completed in eight weeks.

The utility became among the largest companies in Atlantic Canada and was renamed the Nova Scotia Power Corporation. During the energy crisis of the 1970s NSPC counteracted higher oil prices with greater efficiency and by building power plants fuelled by Nova Scotia coal. Construction of the Annapolis tidal power project was completed in 1984, an important step toward fulfilling the dream of producing electricity from the Bay of Fundy.

Nova Scotia Power Corporation's largest generating station—Lingan—the 600-megawatt plant uses 1.6 million tons of coal annually.

FARMERS CO-OPERATIVE DAIRY LIMITED

Selling milk, cream, and other dairy products in Halifax was a simple job at the start of the twentieth century. Milkmen loaded cans of raw milk into horse-drawn wagons, drove to customers' doors, and ladled milk into any container the customer offered. That was how A.D. Johnson started his milk deliveries in Halifax in 1904. Singlehandedly he sold 150 quarts of milk a day to local households and founded a family business called Maple Leaf Dairy. It was a forerunner of Farmers Co-operative Dairy Limited, which is today owned by 275 Nova Scotian dairy farmers and employs over 600 in Atlantic Canada.

During the 1920s processing innovations were beginning to be introduced by local dairies to assure their customers of a safe, nutritious milk supply. The first local dairy to pasteurize—the treatment of raw milk with heat—was Farmers Limited, a company formed in 1922 by a group of dairy farmers. Another innovation that Farmers unveiled by 1938 was an automatic washing machine that allowed the cleaning and filling of glass milk bottles "untouched by hand."

The dairy business thrived for Farmers and Maple Leaf for almost half a century—both companies sold bottled whole milk and cream, plus specialties like buttermilk, cottage cheese, and flavoured ice cream and sherbet. Farmers Limited began delivering its products on Halifax routes using four horse-drawn wagons. The familiar horse-drawn wagons continued until the mid-1950s, when they were finally completely replaced by motorized trucks.

The competing dairies meanwhile coped with processing larger volumes and varieties of milk products. In 1959 Maple Leaf Dairy expanded its Chebucto Road plant by 25 percent. Farmers Limited also grew. By 1961 it covered almost the entire city block at Windsor and North streets and processed some 160,000 pounds of milk each weekday, making it the largest dairy in Eastern Canada.

In 1961 the dairy farmers who supplied milk to Farmers Limited and Maple Leaf Dairy Limited incorporated a co-operative and negotiated the purchase of both

Harold F. Curry, president and general manager of Farmers Co-operative Dairy Limited from 1961 to 1981.

dairies. The co-operative, Twin Cities Co-operative Dairy Limited, was named after the new "twin cities" of Halifax and Dartmouth. The co-operative adopted the familiar Farmers brand name for all of its product lines. In 1983 the now-twenty-year-old firm changed its name to Farmers Co-operative Dairy Limited to better identify the company with its product brand. Today the co-operative business structure assures the continuation of local ownership and control.

Fifteen dairies—from Yarmouth to Truro—joined the co-operative during the 1960s and 1970s as soaring production costs made centralized milk processing a necessity. Regional expansion has followed, with the acquisition of Central Dairies Limited in Newfoundland in 1981.

Farmers revived the Nova Scotia cheese industry, opening a cheddar factory near Truro in 1966. That plant remains the only commercial cheese facility in the province and in 1983 sold almost four million

The deliverymen with their horses and wagons in front of Johnson's Maple Leaf Dairy in 1930 on Chebucto Road in Halifax.

By 1953 trucks had begun to replace horse-drawn vehicles for milk deliveries to Halifax households from Farmers Limited, which was on the corner of Windsor and North streets.

pounds of cheddar throughout Atlantic Canada. After expansion during the 1970s, the cheese factory began making powdered milk. The plant processes most of the province's industrial milk products and annually buys more than thirty-seven million litres of industrial milk from Nova Scotian farmers.

Farmers was the first dairy in Canada to produce spreads that combined butter with margarine (20/80 and 50/50). Another innovation occurred in 1975, when the company opened its ultramodern dairy plant in Bedford, replacing the two older plants in Halifax that had been acquired fourteen years earlier. Covering ninety

acres, the firm's Bedford operation boasts computerized controls, fully automated milk processing, plus energy and water conservation systems. Milk graders and dairy lab chemists constantly monitor product quality.

The latest addition to the Bedford facility is the ultra-high-temperature (UHT) equipment. This modern facility, opened in 1983, produces dairy products with a six-month unrefrigerated shelf life without the use of chemical addi-

tives. Costing more than three million dollars, the UHT facility processes fruit juices as well as milk and is jointly operated by the Farmers and Scotian Gold co-operatives. Since unopened UHT dairy products require no refrigeration, shipping and storage is less costly and more efficient. The co-op is now exporting UHT fluid milk and fruit juices to new markets outside of Canada. Today Farmers Co-operative Dairy Limited's continuing dedication to innovation, product quality, customer service, and community involvement is producing annual sales in excess of eighty-five million dollars, ranking it among the top 500 companies in Canada.

THE HALIFAX HERALD

On January 14, 1875, the first is-sue of the *Morning Herald* was published in Halifax, then a city of 80,000 citizens already served by five daily newspapers. From an of-fice on Bedford Row, *The Herald* first served as a faithful supporter of the Conservative Party. It be-lieved in "the integrity of the Em-pire," the "continuance of the British connection," and solidly endorsed Confederation.

A committee of shareholders operated the paper until 1883, when John James Stewart ac-quired all the shares. In 1897 he sold 50 percent of those holdings to a protégé, William Dennis. Dennis had left England for Nova Scotia in 1870 and, as a seventeen-year-old immigrant, landed a job at *The Herald.* Dennis acquired control of the company in 1907. Five years later he was appointed to the Canadian Senate. After his death in 1920, a majority interest in the firm passed to a nephew, William Henry Dennis, who had

been hired by his uncle in 1900 and worked on the paper as a young jack-of-all-trades. William Henry Dennis, who in 1932 was also made a senator, conducted the affairs of the company until his death in 1954. Control then passed to his son, Graham William Dennis, who remains the present owner,

William Henry Dennis, publisher of The Halifax Herald *from 1920 to 1954.*

chief executive officer, and publish-er of *The Halifax Herald Limited.*

The Herald and its evening com-panion newspaper, *The Mail* (es-tablished in 1879 and published in tandem), thrived over the years. The papers were consistently able to beat the competition with news "scoops" of the day. William Henry Dennis closely linked editorial col-umns and news coverage with the needs of coal miners, fishermen, and farmers in the province. An-other important factor in *The Herald*'s growth was its own circu-lation department.

On January 1, 1949, *The Herald* officially took over its Halifax newspaper rivals, the morning *Chronicle* and the afternoon *Star.* Thus, *The Chronicle-Herald* and *The Mail-Star,* the largest-selling newspapers in Atlantic Canada, were born.

Presiding over *The Halifax Her-ald Limited* for the past thirty years, Graham Dennis has contin-ued the company as an indepen-dent, Nova Scotian enterprise. *The Herald*'s newspapers have a daily circulation of 140,000. Many well-known journalists have served the newspapers, such as Martin Griffin, Snowden Dunn Scott, Charles Hazlitt Cahan, Hiram Wier, R.J. Rankin, W.R. McCurdy, Frank W. Doyle, Donald McRit-chie, James Gowen, and Robert W. Chambers, in the coverage of ma-jor news stories.

The Halifax Herald Limited has always been interested in commu-nity affairs and is active in such organizations as the Rainbow Ha-ven summer camp for children, Goodfellows Club for the needy at Christmas, and the Dalhousie Uni-versity Medical Research Fund.

Robert Chambers (below) whose editorial cartoons were a mainstay of the paper for forty years.

'Mr. Trudeau was right, dear, our lifestyle will be changing.'

H.H. MARSHALL LIMITED

The largest newspaper, magazine, and book distributing business in Atlantic Canada started some eighty years ago when a slight, bespectacled schoolboy named Henry H. Marshall began a newspaper route in Halifax. At the turn of the century the teenaged Marshall saw a future in delivering newspapers quickly, efficiently, and reliably. He acquired a network of city paper routes and hired other boys to make the deliveries. Soon Marshall was responsible for all the major paper routes in Halifax.

By 1914, when his business was formally incorporated as H.H. Marshall Limited, the thirty-year-old Marshall ran three local newsstands (including the first one at the Dartmouth ferry terminal), three other downtown stores, plus a wholesale news depot on Granville Street. Marshall obtained local distribution rights to popular magazines like *The Saturday Evening Post* and sold all kinds of publications—from periodicals and papers to patriotic pamphlets and photo postcards. Helping him as bookkeeper and store manager was his sister, Helen A.B. Marshall. Not one to be idle, Marshall also started a local parcel delivery service to keep his horse-drawn carriages busy during off hours.

In 1918, the year after the great explosion, Henry developed tuberculosis after working as a volunteer on the city's emergency relief commission. As the illness worsened, he could no longer guide his business. Following an unsuccessful recuperative trip to Arizona, H.H. Marshall died in Halifax in 1923.

His sister, Helen, took over the firm and turned the then-faltering operation around with a combination of sharp business sense and a penchant for penny-pinching. She was the first female member of the Halifax Board of Trade and was said to save the string from every newspaper bundle. Under her direction, H.H. Marshall Limited slowly prospered, opening branch offices in Sydney, Nova Scotia, Charlottetown, Prince Edward Island, and St. John's, Newfoundland.

The founder's son, Charles A. Marshall, joined the company in 1945, becoming the second generation in the family business. The 1950s and 1960s saw a rapid increase in the number of magazines published. To keep up with the tons of paper handled daily, the H.H. Marshall Limited headquarters moved to the Halifax north end in 1967. Charles Marshall became company president that same year.

In the 1970s H.H. Marshall Limited expanded again, doubling the size of its Halifax headquarters, modernizing its three branch offices, and starting a regional chain of retail bookstores. As an offshoot, the firm began the Canadiana bookshop, A Pair of Trindles. By the end of the decade H.H. Marshall Limited also started Nimbus Publishing Ltd., a publishing house specializing in Atlantic history, high-quality photography volumes, and regional life-styles.

Throughout the changes, the business remains headed by a Marshall descendant. John Marshall, a grandson of the founder, became president after his father retired in 1982.

Henry H. Marshall, founder and first president of H.H. Marshall Limited, in his Halifax office in 1919.

H.H. Marshall's horse-drawn wagons delivered newspapers, magazines, and parcels throughout Halifax before World War I. This wagon, photographed around 1916 near Marshall's Depot on Granville Street, advertised the publication of Antarctic explorer Captain Robert Scott's diary.

ACADIAN LINES LIMITED

The old bus line headquarters, on Dresden Row in Halifax, was used from 1943 until 1963.

In 1938 Haligonians board an Acadian Lines bus on Spring Garden Road near South Park Street.

Buses in the Maritimes drove into a new era when Acadian Lines Limited, the province's largest highway bus operator, opened its new Halifax terminal in June 1963. "I'm convinced our Almon Street terminal did more than anything else to improve the image of bus travel in Nova Scotia and the whole region," says Acadian Lines president George C. Thompson, who has headed the bus company since it began over forty-six years ago. Acadian Lines' image is a popular one. The firm's blue-and-white buses carry nearly a half-million passengers a year along the 800 miles of routes it operates in Nova Scotia.

It's a long road from 1938, when the bus company started as part of a Maritime gas station, car dealership, and appliance chain. In that era, bus travel was a new and uncertain business. Roads were mostly gravel, buses temperamental, and schedules slow and limited. Initially, for three months Acadian Lines didn't own a single bus but rented them from a competing bus company. Soon Acadian Lines bought four new buses, each one costing $8,500. Those first 26-seater motor coaches were not as

dependable as the more popular trains of that day. But bus travel was less expensive. Haligonians bound for Truro, Antigonish, Sydney, or making connections for New Brunswick and beyond lined up in a garden area beside the Lord Nelson Hotel, at Halifax's first highway bus terminal to wait for those buses. In 1943 Acadian Lines moved to a small, one-storey building on Dresden Row that doubled as a passenger terminal for the next twenty years. From that tiny terminal, general manager George Thompson, his brother Gordon (then Acadian's passenger agent), and Ralph Pepper (traffic manager) concentrated on improving service—running more buses, consolidating routes, adding sightseeing tours, and offering parcel express.

In 1955 the three men bought

Acadian Lines' modern terminal, on Almon Street in Halifax, and its new buses make travel more comfortable.

Acadian Lines after the parent company changed hands. As sole owners, they continued modernizing their buses and terminals. Now with a staff of 145, Acadian Lines celebrated its forty-fifth anniversary in 1983 by purchasing two new, 47-passenger buses, each one air-conditioned, restroom-equipped, and costing $211,000 each. During the past twenty years Acadian Lines has spent more than two million dollars building new bus passenger facilities in Halifax, Truro, Antigonish, and New Glasgow. "We have the best set of bus terminals anywhere in Canada," says George Thompson. He also credits the firm's safe driving record for keeping bus travel popular. In 1983 thirty-one drivers, each logging an average of 50,000 miles annually, received awards for accident-free service.

PATTERSON BROADCASTERS LTD.

The sounds of radio station CFDR were first broadcast from a make-shift studio above a Dartmouth hardware store. That was more than two decades ago, when the station's limited signal sometimes failed to reach outlying parts of Dartmouth. But today CFDR is at the top of both its hometown and its local radio market. The station's call letters shine from atop Dartmouth's tallest building. Inside that office tower, CFDR operates from penthouse studios and enjoys some of the highest radio ratings in the province.

CFDR's easy-listening format makes it the favorite radio station among older adults in the Halifax-Dartmouth area. Now broadcasting with a 50,000-watt signal, the station can reach listeners throughout mainland Nova Scotia.

Founded, owned, and operated by Patterson Broadcasters Ltd., the only independent radio company in metro Halifax, CFDR is also a leader in helping community groups. For organizing a series of successful charity fund-raising events, the station won the Canadian radio industry's Gold Ribbon Award for community service in 1983.

CFDR has developed a large and loyal audience after almost a quarter-century of broadcasting,

C.A. "Arnie" Patterson, president of CFDR and Q-104, began his career as a newspaper reporter and a radio sports commentator and keeps his hand in the business by hosting a sports show and doing a daily news commentary.

according to C.A. "Arnie" Patterson, president of Patterson Broadcasters. "Once people tune into CFDR, they stay there and it becomes a family tradition," he says.

Originally found at 790 on the AM dial, the station was billed as the "Big D" and went on the air December 5, 1962, ceremoniously switched on by Nova Scotia Premier Robert Stanfield. In 1976 CFDR changed its frequency to 680, boosted its broadcasting power, and became the province's first 50,000-watt radio station.

Patterson Broadcasters launched metro's newest music station, Q-104 FM, in October 1983. This time Patterson himself first pushed the on-air button. Although shar-

ing broadcast facilities with CFDR, Q-104 specializes in progressive rock and roll for young listeners. The "Mighty Q" was an immediate success, attracting more than 73,000 weekly listeners within six months of starting. "As far as we can figure, it's the highest first ratings ever for a new FM station in the whole country," says Q-104's news director, Hal Harbour.

Arnie Patterson believes his unlikely combination of radio stations—one for easy listening, the other for hard rock—gives more listeners greater local choice about what they hear on the airwaves. He feels the two sister-stations make Patterson Broadcasters the most successful radio organization in the Maritimes.

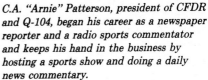

CFDR's twenty-foot neon sign dominates the Dartmouth-Halifax skyline. Perched above eighteen-storey Queen Square, which houses CFDR and its sister-station Q-104, the sign houses a time and temperature board and is a local landmark.

171

BEN'S LTD.

"Ben Moir, Baker, Pepperell St." That simple listing from the 1911 Halifax City Directory remains apt more than seven decades later. Bread wrapped with the Ben's name is still baked on the same street, just south of Quinpool Road. But unlike the original, one-man bakery, today's modern company employs 500 and can produce 5,000 loaves of bread in an hour.

Ben's Ltd. began in the early 1900s following a dispute between two Moir brothers, members of the family running Halifax's then-leading bakery. The Moir business went back to the 1790s, when a Scottish immigrant named Alexander Moir was among the first Halifax bread sellers. By 1815 the baking trade was passed down to Alexander's son. Soon the Moirs' bakery, located at Brunswick and Duke streets, was the town's largest, making bread for Haligonians as well as for the British troops garrisoned at the Citadel.

In 1873 James Moir, the founder's great-grandson, decided to try making candy. His experiments, conducted in a corner of the bakery, led to the addition of sugar almonds, peppermints, and, later, chocolates to the family firm's traditional baked goods.

Although James Moir was a candy maker, when he became company president after 1896, his fussy and frugal manner soured morale in the family firm. Among those who disagreed with James was his younger brother, Ben. As a third-generation baker, Ben Moir

A group of Ben's delivery force poses in front of the firm's Pepperell Street bakery in 1941.

One of the first bread trucks used by Ben's Ltd. around 1930. The boy is helping to deliver bread in the Hydrostone District of Halifax's north end.

prided himself in making the best bread in Halifax. But he disliked working under his overbearing brother. In 1907 the forty-year-old Ben quit the family business and started his own bakery at Shirley and Walnut streets.

Slowly, Ben Moir's operation expanded and moved to larger premises on nearby Pepperell Street, incorporating in August 1913 as Ben Moir Company Ltd. But James Moir, whose business was losing bread sales to brother Ben's bakery, quickly objected to a rival company using the family surname. The next month, Ben Moir simply rechristened his bakery Ben's Ltd., the name that has continued ever since.

The business prospered throughout the 1920s. Cakes, rolls, and pies—even baked beans—were added to the company's product line. Ben Moir visited bakeries throughout North America, keeping an eye on new baking processes and equipment. As his two sons, Robert and Ben Jr., learned the business and helped manage the 75-man operation, Ben Sr. found more time for his Stutz automobiles and marathon poker games.

Beginning in 1926, a series of misfortunes hit the company. In February of that year, the Ben's bakery on Pepperell Street burned to the ground. With the help of substantial bank loans, the bakery was rebuilt and back in business

A familiar sight to Haligonians was Ben's fleet of horse-drawn delivery vehicles. Photo circa 1948

within four months, complete with the latest ovens and machinery. The new equipment allowed Ben's Ltd. to expand into the canning business—processing more baked bean products, even foxberry jelly—while increasing its line of bakery goods.

The next difficulty proved more serious. When the Depression hit four years later, the bakery still owed $250,000 from reconstruction costs. The debt drove Ben's Ltd. to the brink of bankruptcy in 1932.

As a last-ditch effort to prevent foreclosure, the bakery's creditors called for a change in the firm's management and placed Robert Moir, the eldest son of Ben Sr., in charge. Then came a double setback. Robert died unexpectedly in 1934, soon followed by the death of Ben Sr. The task of running the near-bankrupt bakery fell to 34-year-old Ben Moir, Jr. By emphasizing quality and proper accounting, Ben Jr. got the bakery out of debt and in 1935 posted a $13,000 profit on sales of $330,000. He toured the plant daily, testing the bread and looking for better baking methods. He was among the first bakers in Canada to install automated pie- and doughnut-

making machines. By 1939 Ben's bread was the largest-selling brand in Nova Scotia, with sales totalling more than $500,000.

Throughout World War II and later, Ben's Ltd. was hampered by rationed supplies, lack of equipment, and insufficient personnel. Production of canned beans ended in 1940 due to shortages of tin and produce. Six years later continuing sugar rationing forced the bakery to stop making all sweet goods. To make up for lost sales of cakes and cookies, Ben Jr. decided to expand bread production. By 1948 freshly baked loaves and rolls were shipped throughout Nova Scotia and New

Brunswick using a distribution network of trains and the firm's fleet of ten delivery trucks. Business continued to thrive during the 1950s, with the exception of a bitter labour strike at the bakery in 1957. In that decade more than

An artist's view of Ben's Pepperell Street bakery in the 1950s.

two million dollars was spent expanding and modernizing the bakery, and the staff grew to more than 125 workers.

The 1960s marked a new era for Ben's Ltd. After running the business for nearly thirty years, Ben Moir, Jr., then sixty-one, sold the bakery to Nova Scotia industrialist Roy Jodrey in 1961. Ironically, a few years earlier, Jodrey had purchased Moir's Ltd., the family business Ben Moir, Sr., had left a half-century before. For six years the once-rival Halifax bakeries amalgamated and produced a full line of breads, doughnuts, cakes, and sweets. In 1967 Jodrey sold the confectionery operation and the Moir's candy trademarks to Standard Brands (now Nabisco Brands).

Ben Moir, Jr., died in 1973, but the bakery his father started remains among the most modern in Canada, continuing to grow as part of the Jodrey family interests. Ben's Ltd. currently sells baked goods in all three Maritime provinces, and has acquired bakeries in Dartmouth and Moncton, New Brunswick.

THE MARITIME LIFE ASSURANCE COMPANY

In an industry known for its conservative nature, the Halifax-based Maritime Life Assurance Company has enjoyed rapid growth in the past decade by being just the opposite. Largely through innovative insurance ideas, such as linking policies to investment opportunities, sixty-year-old Maritime Life is now among Canada's most important life insurance companies.

Maritime Life was incorporated in 1922, when an estimated ten million dollars in life insurance premiums left the Maritimes annually. The aim of the firm was to reverse that trend—catering to the life insurance needs of Maritimers, while keeping insurance premiums in Eastern Canada as investments. Although Maritime Life's operations now extend across Canada, the company remains committed to the East Coast with some $154 million invested in the region. Maritime Life, with its modern, mirrored-glass headquarters overlooking Halifax's Northwest Arm, is the only national life insurer in the country based east of Quebec City.

Maritime Life first opened for business with a staff of six, working from an office in the Dennis Building on Granville Street. By 1925 some 547 insurance contracts, worth more than one million dollars, were in effect. During those early years other Maritime Life offices opened in Moncton, New Brunswick, and Charlottetown, Prince Edward Island, plus agencies were established in Bermuda, the West Indies, and the then-British colony of Newfoundland. Ten years later insurance policies worth thirteen million dollars were written by Maritime Life staff. The increased business forced the firm to move to larger premises. During World War II insurance business continued to grow, but

Maritime Life's operations were hampered by the loss of key personnel to the armed forces. In 1944 a fire destroyed the building that housed Maritime Life's headquarters. Fortunately, all insurance records were salvaged, but the company faced the difficult task of finding new offices in a city congested by wartime activity. Maritime Life moved into temporary offices until a permanent home was found—a one-time burlesque theatre on Sackville Street near Barrington that was renovated for business use.

Another corporate move occurred thirteen years later, when Maritime Life built its own headquarters on Spring Garden Road. The building opened in 1954, the year Maritime Life's insurance policies were valued at more than forty-five million dollars. The firm then set its sights westward and operations expanded into Ontario and Quebec, the first step to becoming a national insurer. Sales in the 1960s paved the way for rapid future growth, thanks to three factors—Maritime Life's reliance on independent agents to sell its policies, rather than setting up branch offices throughout the country; the company's early automation of bookkeeping records, beginning in 1956; and the development of a special division to provide insurance for Canadian armed forces personnel in both Canada and Europe.

Between 1956 and 1966 Maritime Life expanded faster than any other life insurance company in Canada. To maintain such growth, especially with new Canadian tax laws adopted in 1968, the firm needed further financial support. In 1969 Maritime Life became a wholly owned subsidiary of The John Hancock Mutual Life Insurance Company, one of the

largest life insurers. Based in Boston, Hancock provided money and technical help to further increase Maritime Life's business. But Maritime Life was to remain true to its name. As a Hancock executive noted at the time of the takeover: "If we are going to write insurance in Halifax, let's have it written in Halifax. Let Halifax have the tax on earnings held . . . in Halifax. Let's have Halifax people trained to do the best job here."

That commitment was reinforced in 1973. On Maritime Life's fiftieth anniversary, the firm opened its present headquarters on Dutch Village Road. Growth continued, thanks to new types of insurance policies offered by Maritime Life. Many of these ideas were subsequently adopted by competing businesses. In 1984 Maritime Life's assets reached $1.35 billion, more than five times its business in 1978. The number of individual policies in force nearly doubled in that period—to 130,000 in 1984 compared to 70,000 in 1978. Employer group insurance has enjoyed similar growth. Maritime Life has also recently expanded its pension fund activities for groups.

One of Maritime Life's future goals is to become the leading life insurer of Atlantic Canadians. The East Coast is Maritime Life's fastest-growing base of business and an important market. In 1984 the firm had eighty million dollars of assets invested in Nova Scotia, following Maritime Life's ongoing policy of closely matching investments to its obligations to policyholders in the province.

Maritime Life's attractive national headquarters building, overlooking Halifax's Northwest Arm, was completed in 1973 to accommodate the firm's rapid expansion.

I.H. MATHERS & SON LIMITED

"The fine new brigantine, *Lady Josvan,* will be dispatched from Liverpool on 23rd May for this port," announced a small shipping notice in the Halifax *Morning Chronicle,* May 30, 1872. "For freight and other particulars, apply . . . in Halifax to Isaac H. Mathers." The *Lady Josvan* is now long forgotten, but not the shipping agent's company. More than a century after Isaac H. Mathers opened his office in a Halifax warehouse beside a waterfront coal depot, I.H. Mathers & Son Limited remains family owned and recognized by shippers and mariners throughout the world.

Headquartered in Mathers House, a modern Halifax office building, the firm is run by the founder's great-grandson, Harry Isaac Mathers III, and continues Isaac H. Mathers' work—looking after the cargoes and crews of vessels in port. What started as a one-man business now employs fifty

The 343-ton schooner Helen Mathers *was purchased by the firm in 1919 and operated in the United Kingdom and Caribbean trades.*

office staff and some 300 more personnel at sea. The company currently operates a group of ocean-related businesses, including one of Canada's oldest travel agencies, a crewing and stevedore service, marine brokerage, and a fleet of supply vessels for oil and gas exploration off the East Coast.

The firm's story began in 1870, when Isaac Mathers said goodbye to his home in Newry, Northern Ireland, joined a Liverpool-based shipping company, and sailed to New York City. There, he started a shipping office for his employer, then went to Saint John, New Brunswick, the next year and opened a Canadian branch. When he arrived in Halifax in 1872, Mathers stayed and set up his own business.

In those days Halifax Harbour was a forest of sailing masts, and competition between shipping agents was fierce. To obtain an advantage, Mathers posted a man on Citadel Hill to watch for incoming ships. When one was spotted, the lookout ran to dockside, rowed out to the approaching ship, and bar-

Isaac H. Mathers (1835-1932), founder.

gained with the captain to appoint Mathers as agent. Many agreed, and Mathers' company flag, a black "M" on a white square with a green background, became a well-known sight flying from Citadel Hill's commercial signal mast.

Mathers, who was joined in business in 1890 by his son, Harry Isaac, also exported Nova Scotia lumber and canned lobster. Company records from 1898 show that Mathers bought more than 26,000 pounds of canned lobster meat, priced at about twenty cents a pound, destined for overseas palates. During this time Isaac H. Mathers applied to the governments of Denmark, Norway, and Sweden and was appointed the local diplomatic representative for those countries.

His son, Harry, later became vice-consul for Czarist Russia. (Harry's application for that diplomatic post, sent in January 1899, included a letter of recommendation from the premier of Nova Scotia.) After the Russian Revolu-

Eastern Trust with eleven more branches and an entrée to the Ontario market. By 1981, as assets reached $1.9 billion, the corporate name was simplified to Central Trust Company. Two years later Central Trust assumed the management of Crown Trust Company, which added eleven branches in Quebec, Ontario, and the West. By 1985 Central Trust operated fifty-seven branches across the country, from St. John's, Newfoundland, to Victoria, British Columbia, and employed more than 1,200.

This expansion provided customers with a broader range of services. For example, in 1980 Central Trust was the first Canadian trust company to offer Visa credit cards. Also, new computerized systems allow faster and better financial arrangements for both individual and corporate customers. Meanwhile, Central Trust continues to operate its own real estate brokerage service in the Atlantic region.

Recently, a corporate donation was made in recognition of the Nova Scotia government's procurement of a copy of the province's first charter. Dated 1621 and written in Latin, the parchment records how King James I granted Nova Scotia and adjacent lands to a Scottish nobleman for colonization. Construction of Central Trust's modern Halifax headquarters revealed another chapter of the city's history. Excavation at the building's downtown site uncovered more than 20,000 artifacts dating to the original settlement of Halifax more than two centuries ago.

An artist's rendition of the Central Trust Tower, Halifax, which opened in the spring of 1985. The head office of the company and a full-service branch occupies the tower.

THE BANK OF NOVA SCOTIA

The head office building of The Bank of Nova Scotia, constructed in 1931, remains today on Hollis Street, Halifax.

The group of prominent Nova Scotians who gathered at the Merchants Exchange Coffee House in Halifax in December 1831 had more in mind than casual discussion of the day's shipping reports. They were there to solve one of the colony's most pressing problems: the need for a people's bank.

The early 1830s were years of growth and promise for Nova Scotia. Farming, fishing, shipbuilding, and trade formed solid cornerstones for the area's economy. But as commerce grew, so did the frustration of merchants and businessmen trying to cope with the increasing inadequacy of the colony's monetary and financial facilities.

Cash was in chronic short supply. Heavy import demands tended to drain off reserves as soon as they were earned. Even when available, what passed for legal currency was often such a confusing variety of foreign coin that the simplest transactions became complicated and time consuming.

An equal source of frustration to many Nova Scotians was the Halifax Banking Company, a privately owned firm with virtual control over the colony's financial services.

Determined to compete against this monopoly, William Lawson, a Halifax businessman and representative in the House of Assembly, organized other influential citizens to develop the colony's first public bank. Included in the group were W.B. Bliss, who would soon be appointed to the Nova Scotia Supreme Court; James W. Johnston, an important Conservative who would one day be premier of the province; and James Boyle Uniacke, a lawyer who later became attorney general of Nova Scotia.

Just four months after their first meeting at the Merchants Exchange, the men won House of Assembly approval to form a public bank. Directors were elected, and on March 30, 1832, The Bank of Nova Scotia was incorporated as the first chartered bank in the colony.

Five months later the bank opened the doors of its Granville Street, Halifax, office to the public. With a staff of four, it offered authorized capital of 100,000 pounds.

Though this was perhaps a modest beginning, The Bank of Nova Scotia's early endeavours were neither provincial nor routine. Founded in a seaport town by merchants and traders with an entrepreneurial spirit and an explorer's sense of adventure, the bank participated from the outset in the most dynamic aspects of Nova Scotia commerce.

Since those early days Halifax has occupied a special place in The Bank of Nova Scotia's traditions and in its present-day operations. Halifax remains the home of Scotiabank's head office building, located on Hollis Street, and is the location of the bank's annual meeting of shareholders.

Today Scotiabank is a recognized financial leader throughout the world, with close to 1,200 offices and branches located in fifty-two countries. Together with Jack Keith, regional senior vice-president and general manager, Nova Scotia Region, The Bank of Nova Scotia and its staff take great pleasure in recognizing the special contribution of Halifax to its worldwide operations, and look forward to many more years of growth and prosperity in the city.

The Halifax main branch, located at street level in the Hollis Street facility, retains the detailed beauty of architect John Lyle's original design.

DOANE RAYMOND

Canada's only major chartered accounting firm based outside of Toronto or Montreal started in Halifax more than forty-five years ago. While retaining its head office in Halifax, Doane Raymond (formerly H.R. Doane and Company) has expanded operations into eight provinces and become part of an international chartered accounting network represented in more than fifty countries.

Harvey R. Doane was the managing partner of the accounting company until 1963. During his career the firm opened offices in all four Atlantic provinces and grew to have fourteen partners. After Doane retired, Calvin A. Rice was appointed executive partner, a position he still holds. Under his direction, the firm expanded within the Atlantic provinces and moved westward, reaching Ontario, Manitoba, Alberta, and British Columbia. Currently Doane Raymond has more than 100 partners and operates thirty-five offices in Canada.

Doane Raymond's range of professional services has also increased. With a focus on small and medium-size businesses, the organization provides services in ac-

Partners on the firm's National Management Committee are (seated, left to right) Roland S. Jamieson, Glenn R. Williams, Allan Berkshire, Calvin A. Rice, H. Larry Doane, chairman, Allister R. Byrne, Carman R. Colwell, and John E. Gover; (standing, left to right) Ralph L. Sykes and C. William Hayward.

counting, auditing, management consulting, and tax planning to thousands of clients. In addition to private business, Doane Raymond works with various levels of government and public agencies. The firm has also introduced computerized accounting systems to make financial record keeping faster and easier.

Added to this professional expertise, Doane Raymond partners are active in community service throughout Canada. The tradition began with Harvey Doane, who was a leader in Kiwanis, Canadian Red Cross, the Canadian Bible Society, and Scottish Rite. In Halifax, company partners now holding notable community positions include Keith Thompson, chairman of the Izaak Walton Killam Hospital for Children; H. Larry Doane,

chairman of The Canadian Tax Foundation; and C. William Hayward, president of the Halifax Club.

Doane Raymond's tradition of service to the profession is also strong. In 1950 Harvey Doane headed the national Chartered Accountants' Association, a position since held by three other Doane Raymond partners—Harold A. Renouf, Randolph W. Manning, and H. Larry Doane. Calvin Rice was the first of a number of the firm's partners to become chairman of the Atlantic Provinces Association of Chartered Accountants, a group that provides special-education programs for chartered accountant students throughout the region.

Across Canada, Doane Raymond's staff numbers over 600, with about a third of its personnel in Nova Scotia. The Halifax-based firm is represented in Quebec by that province's largest accounting company. The Doane Raymond offices are in Halifax's Scotia Square. Working in the Halifax area are twenty-five partners and a staff of more than 100 metro residents.

SEAMAN CROSS LIMITED

Fifty years ago an enterprise was launched by Colonel L.N. Seaman that would become Atlantic Canada's largest office furniture and equipment supplier. Within months Seaman formed a partnership with Captain Paul B. Cross, and they operated from an office on Granville Street. When World War II commenced Cross was called for active duty, leaving his older partner to manage the business for the next six years. Despite the wartime shortage, Seaman kept the business operating by training women as repair technicians.

After the war Cross decided against returning to the business he had co-founded. However, his nephew, Flying Officer William Cross Kitchen, following service in the RCAF, was hired by Seaman. The staff of six sold and serviced typewriters and other business machines throughout the region. Due to poor health, Seaman retired and sold the company in 1947 to Kitchen and retired RCAF Officer William Mighell. They ran the concern together until Kitchen became president and sole owner in 1955.

During that time Seaman Cross expanded into office furniture sales. Business thrived, and in 1957 the company opened a larger headquarters on Barrington Street— a building designed as a showcase for its sales and services. The firm was the first in Atlantic Canada to establish its own interior design department.

In 1962 Seaman Cross Limited completed what was then its largest contract—supplying two floors of office furnishings for Halifax's first modern skyscraper, the eight-storey Canada Permanent Build-

Seaman Cross Limited began at this Granville Street location, where the firm remained until 1957.

ing. Since then other notable local projects for Seaman Cross have included furnishing libraries, supplying auditorium seats at Neptune Theatre, furnishing offices and residences at Dalhousie University, and equipping the Victoria General Hospital with hospital furnishings.

The company was one of the first to move into the next new development in Halifax: The Trade Mart, Scotia Square, in 1963. Seaman Cross then added carpeting and drapery departments to provide a complete range of office furnishings. Six years later the firm again needed a larger home

and moved to its present location in Dartmouth's Burnside Industrial Park.

Kitchen sold the business in 1976 to two senior employees, his nephew, David McCormack, and George MacKay. The new owners retained Kitchen as president and opened a branch office in New Brunswick. Staff at Seaman Cross Limited currently numbers seventy-five, including equipment consultants, designers, and technicians.

The Burnside Industrial Park has been the site of Seaman Cross Limited since 1969.

HALIFAX INDUSTRIES LIMITED

Blasted out of solid rock, the first Halifax shipyard took shape in 1889 to serve Queen Victoria's Royal Navy. The original 567-foot-long graving dock was used for cleaning and patching wooden hulls of naval and merchant ships. Today the almost-century-old dry dock is part of a modern ship-building and -repair complex spread across sixty acres on both sides of the harbour. The deep-water and ice-free port of Halifax is an ideal location for such work. Beside the facility is CFB Halifax, Canada's largest East Coast naval base. Also, the transatlantic shipping route is nearby, as are Nova Scotia's fishing grounds and off-shore natural gas fields. All have contributed to the growth and development of the two local shipyards, one in Halifax, the other in Dartmouth.

The Dartmouth Marine Slips were established in 1859, but ship repair and construction began on that sandy, sheltered beach site as early as 1785. Canada's first marine railway was built at the Dartmouth slips in 1860. Four such railways are now used there. Across the harbour, the Halifax yard became a private business by 1915. Two years later the Halifax explosion flattened every building at the shipyard. However, the graving dock remained undamaged and the firm resumed operation. By the 1930s the Dominion Steel and Coal Corporation (Dosco) ran and began expanding both the Halifax Shipyards Limited and the Dartmouth Marine Slips.

During World War II the two shipyards worked around the clock. Workers repaired more than 7,200 ships—from battleships to small merchant freighters—damaged in the North Atlantic convoys. The Halifax yard also designed and constructed the first

Opened in 1889 as part of the Naval Dock-yard, the graving dock is shown here with the first ship to be dry-docked. In 1918 this facility was taken over by Halifax Industries Limited.

naval destroyers built in the country.

Canada's Navy remained an important customer for the shipyards after the war. Three Royal Canadian Navy antisubmarine escorts were constructed at the Halifax yard during the 1950s. Today both shipyards repair and refit other Canadian naval vessels—from destroyers to submarines.

From the late 1950s until 1978, Hawker-Siddeley Canada Ltd. operated the Dartmouth and Halifax facilities. The shipyards built twenty-six fishing trawlers, then constructed seven semisubmersible drilling rigs, the first such vessels ever made in Canada. Ownership of the two yards then passed to a specially formed partnership, Halifax Industries Limited, until 1984.

With the worldwide collapse of the shipbuilding industry during the late 1970s, the Halifax yard

An aerial view of the Dartmouth Marine Slips.

moved into more diversified markets, such as ship repair and conversions. Thanks to the financial backing of the Nova Scotia government, the yards acquired a $63-million floating dry dock in 1983 and have continued operating despite difficult economic conditions.

WOOD MOTORS FORD LIMITED

Wood Motors Ford Limited celebrated its fiftieth birthday in 1984 by becoming the top-selling Ford dealership in Canada. More than 2,300 new vehicles were sold in 1984 and gross sales were almost thirty-seven million dollars. That a company in the Maritimes could surpass the more than 700 other Ford dealerships in the country surprised many industry officials. But not John Gwynne-Timothy, president and owner of Wood Motors Ford. "It's a story of continued growth because we've received a lot of support not only from the Halifax-Dartmouth area, but from all over the province," he says.

Gwynne-Timothy started selling cars as a teenager in Halifax in 1963. His strong sales record with different dealers soon attracted national attention. By 1968 the 24-year-old, ex-professional golfer was one of metro's top car salesmen. He later spent four successful years in real estate sales and management, then returned to an automotive career. In 1977 Gwynne-

John Gwynne-Timothy, president and owner.

Timothy bought his first car dealership and in twenty-one months turned what had been a bankrupt car sales company into a thriving enterprise.

When Gwynne-Timothy sold that Dartmouth dealership he expected to retire. But the car business called him back. In 1979 the Wood Motors Ford dealership was for sale and Gwynne-Timothy bought it. The firm was then

ranked fifty-sixth among Ford dealers in Canada. "I certainly had no aspirations at that time," he recalls.

But Gwynne-Timothy recognized the dealership's potential. It is among the oldest Ford affiliates in the region, tracing its roots back to a company called Universal Sales, begun in April 1934. First located on Brenton Street in south end Halifax, the dealership was originally part of a transportation-related group of companies. By the 1940s the growing Universal Sales car business needed more space for its vehicles and took over the old south end skating rink at South and Fenwick streets.

World War II halted car manufacturing and made buying and selling new vehicles impossible. But Universal Sales stayed in business and kept a stockpile of cars reserved for emergency use at its rink building. If Halifax police or national defence personnel needed a vehicle, they went to Universal's warehouse, called the city's car

The north end intersection of Windsor Street and Kempt Road, one of the busiest spots in Halifax, has been the site of Wood Motors since 1968.

pound, and signed out a car for temporary use.

In January 1953 Universal Sales was bought by Fredericton businessman Bliss Wood, a Ford dealer in the New Brunswick capital. The company name was changed and has remained Wood Motors Ford. Wood's partner in the car business was K.C. Irving, founder of the Irving Oil Company and owner of a wide range of New Brunswick-based businesses.

By 1959 Wood Motors in Halifax employed seventy-five people, including fifteen salesmen. The expanding company kept about seventy new cars and 170 used vehicles in stock at a number of Halifax locations—at the main office on Brenton Street, two car lots on South Street, and another lot in the north end at Windsor and Young streets. The firm consolidated operations in 1961, building a new headquarters, showroom, and garage at the old south end rink site. Seven years later Wood Motors moved completely across the city, to its present north end location at the corner of Windsor Street and Kempt Road.

Wood Motors was the number one Ford dealer in Canada in 1984 and was awarded the Dealer Distinguished Achievement Award for the fourth consecutive year. Making the presentation to John Gwynne-Timothy is Jim O'Connor, vice-president of sales and marketing, Ford of Canada.

Attending the 1984 award celebration are (from left to right) His Worship Ronald Wallace, mayor of Halifax; the Honourable Alan Abraham, lieutenant-governor of the province of Nova Scotia; and the Honourable John Buchanan, premier of the province of Nova Scotia.

Owner Gwynne-Timothy credits that site for much of the dealership's success. The north end intersection is one of Halifax's busiest, with more than 40,000 cars passing the Wood Motors' sign and showroom every weekday. "It has a strategic location; we've got a lot of good people and sound marketing techniques," Gwynne-Timothy explains.

The change in management got results. One month in the summer of 1981, Wood Motors ranked first in Ford car sales for Canada. That was considered a major achievement since the Halifax-Dartmouth automobile market is ranked tenth in size nationally. Also, the metro market is very competitive, with one car dealer for every 5,500 people in Halifax, compared to one dealer for every 10,000 Ontario residents.

But Wood Motors' sales success continued. In the first three months of 1983, the firm sold more cars than any other Ford dealer in the country, an honour usually won by dealers in larger centres such as Toronto, Montreal, or Calgary. The Halifax dealership regularly placed first in monthly Ford

sales Canada-wide and became a contender for the annual top spot. Among the country's Ford dealers, Wood Motors ranked tenth in overall sales in 1981, climbed to sixth place the next year, and placed third in 1983. The Halifax dealership then captured the yearly sales title in 1984, beating its closest rival by fifty-five cars.

With ninety-five employees, including a 21-member sales staff, Wood Motors' current annual payroll is $3.5 million. The dealership's advertising budget in 1984 exceeded $700,000, the largest of any Canadian Ford dealer. Local reports describe Gwynne-Timothy

The Wood Motors Ford Limited showroom.

as a "complete salesman, a marketer nonparalleled in . . . one of the most competitive businesses in Canada." He is also one of the most community-minded. Wood Motors Ford is a major supporter of local and national charitable groups and nonprofit organizations. "We just want to continue to supply fair prices and strong service in the marketplace," explains Gwynne-Timothy.

187

MARITIME PAPER PRODUCTS LTD.

Such diverse Nova Scotia products as apples, fresh fish, and bottled beer are all packed in boxes made by Maritime Paper Products Ltd., the province's first and only corrugated container manufacturer. Maritime Paper began making cardboard cartons in north end Halifax during the Depression more than fifty years ago. Starting a business then was a huge risk, yet there was a growing demand for corrugated boxes. The biggest customers were the region's breweries which, as liquor laws relaxed after Prohibition, needed more cartons to ship their products.

William H.C. Schwartz, then president of his family's spice company, W.H. Schwartz and Sons Ltd., recognized that a paper products firm could be a success in Halifax. He persuaded other businessmen, including Halifax brewer Sidney C. Oland, to help organize Maritime Paper Products. To reduce start-up costs, the company used second-hand machinery in its newly built factory on Almon Street. That equipment, with modifications, kept operating for the next seventeen years. The firm hired its first workers at the hourly wage of thirty cents for men, eighteen cents for women, and production began on July 6, 1931. Although all jobs were filled by that opening day, more than 200 people crowded outside Maritime Paper's factory still hoping for work. During its first years Maritime Paper Products survived thanks to regional cooperation. Users of corrugated paper in the Maritimes bought solely from the Halifax-based concern to keep needed jobs in the region.

During World War II, few men were available for factory labour. To maintain production, Maritime Paper relied on women to do heavy manual jobs which, accord-

Maritime Paper Products Ltd.'s original factory on Almon Street, west of Robie Street.

ing to corporate records, "never before were considered suitable for female workers." In 1948 Maritime Paper expanded and new machines were installed. The firm produced innovative corrugated apple and strawberry containers, which were destined to replace costly wooden barrels and boxes. Maritime Paper also designed strong, wax-impregnated corrugated cartons for food processing. These products remain an important part of the business.

Roy Jodrey's Minas Basin Pulp and Power Company bought Maritime Paper Products in 1958. Under this ownership, which continues today, the paper products firm expanded again with more staff and equipment. By 1961 the company could produce twenty-five miles of corrugated paper in a nine-hour shift. Seeing more production, and with expansion impossible at the Halifax site, in 1967 Maritime Paper Products moved into a modern $4.5-million factory built in Dartmouth. The firm was among the first to locate in the Burnside Industrial Park. Subsequent improvements at the Dartmouth plant now allow Maritime Paper Products' staff of 200 to make 3.5 million square feet of corrugated paper a day, enough to serve customers throughout Atlantic Canada, west to Ontario and overseas.

The current headquarters of Maritime Paper Products is in Dartmouth's Burnside Industrial Park.

VOLVO CANADA LTD.

A part of Scandinavia came to Nova Scotia in 1963 when Volvo, the Swedish automaker, opened its first North American car assembly factory on the Dartmouth side of Halifax Harbour.

Volvo, a company that began in 1927 and now annually makes about 325,000 cars worldwide, found the Canadian East Coast site ideal. Metro Halifax offered direct shipping links to Volvo's headquarters in southern Sweden, an ice-free port for year-round transport of car parts, and a skilled local work force. Since June 11, 1963, when the first Canadian-built Volvo rolled off the assembly line, the company's operations have remained at near capacity. Volvo's growth in Canada was so rapid during the early 1960s that the firm's Dartmouth factory soon proved too small. In 1967 Volvo moved across the harbour to a larger assembly plant on Halifax's Pier 9, which has since been expanded twice. In 1984 more than 10,000 cars were assembled in Halifax, part of the total 170,000 Volvos assembled during the past two decades.

The Halifax production begins with uncrating the painted body prior to its start down the assembly line. One of the first stations the car encounters supplies it with its serial number and other documentation that accompanies the car through a long line of eighty assembly stations encompassing over 3,000 parts. Although workers generally build from complete components, they are also required to construct such assemblies as complete seats and backrests in various colors and materials (work

Phase one of assembly operation.

done by a separate upholstery plant for the European plants).

In addition to this, the assembly includes such major jobs as engine subassembly and a thorough undercoating of the car. The plant has recently added an innovative method of tilting the car at various stations to install gas tanks and lines, and to undercoat the body. The plant, with its experienced work force, has in recent years met all of Volvo's worldwide quality standards and, in fact, had the highest quality audit in 1984.

Officials at Volvo Canada Ltd., a subsidiary of the parent Swedish company, are proud of the Halifax assembly plant. "It's rated number one in efficiency," says a Volvo spokesman. "There are only about forty-five cars made in Halifax a day and the quality of those cars is very high." Plant management points to consistently excellent productivity due to good workmanship and good workers. While the automotive industry is known for its frequent layoffs, turnover among the 180 employees at Volvo's Halifax plant is low—the average employee has worked there for more than ten years.

This is the marriage point—the body is elevated to the high-line for installation of the engine, transmission, front and rear suspension, and axle.

MOIRS DIVISION, NABISCO BRANDS LTD.

Thanks to James Moir, the sweet smell of chocolate drifted over downtown Halifax for more than a century. In 1873 he began experimenting with various mixtures of chocolate and candy in his family's bakery near Citadel Hill. The idea of making sweets was not altogether new to the Moir business. For three previous generations the Moirs had baked bread and cakes, and even built the largest bakery in Halifax. But mass-producing chocolates was an entirely different process. James Moir spent long

Moirs Ltd. as it looked on March 2, 1927.

The firm was still at the same location but had undergone extensive renovation before the property was sold and a new chocolate-making factory opened in 1975.

hours in a corner of his father's bakery trying to perfect various candy recipes. The story is told of how he often sampled his day's work from atop Citadel Hill. His goal was to produce the finest chocolate in North America.

Success came for James Moir after twenty years of testing when he created the special XXX blend of chocolate. His recipe is still used today. As a seaport, Halifax was ideal for a chocolate-manufacturing business since ingredients came from such far-off places as Central and South America, Indonesia, China, India, Africa, and Europe. By the 1890s, when James Moir

became head of the family business, he was selling his sweets across Canada and beyond.

A disastrous fire in 1903 destroyed the entire family enterprise, including the bakery, candy machines, and paper box factory. Three hundred people were put out of work. Undaunted, James Moir rebuilt and resumed production. During the 1920s the Moir business was reorganized and thrived. More than 1,000 workers made chocolates and cakes, bread and biscuits from what was then among the most modern factories in Canada. Staff worked ten-hour shifts, and experienced people, mostly women, received twenty-five cents an hour. The company introduced its Pot of Gold boxed chocolates in 1928, a brand that remains a best-seller two generations later.

With a strong emphasis on candy making, Moirs Ltd. stayed in the family until 1957 when the company was sold to a group of Maritime businessmen. During the next decade the forty-year-old factory was updated with millions of dollars worth of new equipment. Sales rose 60 percent. Moirs was one of the first candy manufactur-

Today Moirs is a division of Nabisco Brands Ltd. and is located in this ultra-modern facility in Dartmouth.

ers to use clear cellophane wrapping to keep its boxed chocolates fresh. But rising ingredient prices and increased competition prevented Moirs from continuing as a locally owned company. In 1967 Moirs' candy division was sold to Standard Brands (now Nabisco Brands Ltd.). Under new ownership, the Moirs name was retained, the old downtown Halifax property sold, and a new chocolate-making factory opened in Dartmouth in 1975. The 350 workers at the Dartmouth facility now make more than two million boxes of Moirs' Pot of Gold chocolates each year, as well as the other lines of boxed chocolates.

MONTREAL TRUST

Since Montreal Trust came to Halifax almost eighty years ago, the full-service trust company has forged strong links with customers throughout Nova Scotia and the Atlantic region. Now corporately known as Montreal Trustco Inc., it is among Canada's largest trust companies, with more than twenty billion dollars worth of assets under administration. "Our strength lies in the traditional trust fields, but we are continually expanding our services to cover all our clients' financial needs," explains Ross Pritchard, vice-president and manager of Montreal Trust's Halifax office. With three offices and eighty staff members in metro, Montreal Trust provides individuals and businesses with a wide range of investment, trust, and real estate services.

The firm was originally incorporated in 1889 as the Montreal Safety Deposit Company and chose Halifax for its first branch office some two decades later. In 1907 a businessman named Maxwell Aitken left Halifax to become managing director of Montreal Trust. Aitken, who would later immigrate to Britain and receive the title of Lord Beaverbrook, paved the way for Montreal Trust's arrival in Halifax by negotiating its acquisition of a local financial firm.

After being registered in Nova Scotia in 1912, Montreal Trust opened an office at Hollis and George streets, later moving to the building next door. During those early years the company emphasized personal trust services, including planning and managing estates.

Halifax branch managers were often prominent local businessmen, who played a leading role in the community. Also, the company formed advisory boards to provide

Montreal Trust's quarters were located in the historic Queen Building, at Prince and Hollis streets, from 1954 until 1975.

advice and counsel to local senior management. This practice continues today, with the six-member Halifax board one of Montreal Trust's four such groups in Atlantic Canada.

Local business grew and in 1954 the company bought the historic Queen Building at Prince and Hollis streets for its Halifax branch. Montreal Trust won an award for its restoration of the cream-coloured building, a city landmark since 1867. The provincial government later took over the structure and in 1975 the trust company moved across Hollis Street, into its present offices in the modern Joseph Howe Building.

Since the 1950s the Montreal-based trust company has greatly expanded its financial services for business and personal accounts. Locally, Montreal Trust arranged the $4.5-million financing for Halifax's Park Victoria apartment building in 1964, then the largest residential mortgage ever granted in Atlantic Canada. The trust com-

In 1975 the trust company moved across Hollis Street into its present offices in the Joseph Howe Building.

pany, a subsidiary of the Power Corporation of Canada, now has more than 250,000 individual customers across the country. Montreal Trust is also a recognized leader in corporate financial services, providing stock transfer, corporate trust, and pension services to many of Canada's major corporations.

THE HALIFAX INSURANCE COMPANY

"Fire and destruction were as possible as catching a cold" during the early 1800s in Halifax, according to one local newspaper report. In those days most of the inhabitants in the British colonial seaport lived and worked in crudely heated wooden buildings. Protection against fire was equally primitive. "Early Halifax had the water bucket and the ax—that was about all" was one description of early fire-fighting equipment. Accord-

ingly, fire insurance in the Nova Scotia capital was high-priced and often impossible to obtain from local agents of British or American insurers. That changed in the spring of 1809, after seven Haligonians met in the popular Exchange Coffee House on Upper Water Street. The men agreed to form what was to be Canada's first insurance business—the Halifax Fire Insurance Association, forerunner of today's Halifax Insurance Company.

The association started with one employee, the secretary/treasurer who worked from a single room in his Hollis Street home. A cedar shingle with the hand-lettered words "Fire Insurance" hung outside his door. The appearance of this home-grown insurer had a sudden effect on underwriting in

Halifax. Within ten weeks insurance rates from competing firms began to drop for the first time in Halifax's sixty-year history. Company records show the fledgling Halifax Fire Insurance Association suffered no losses during its early years. Such good fortune and sound management for the next decade allowed the business to enlarge and incorporate.

Halifax Fire Insurance provided important community services during that era. Halifax's first fire engine—a water pump on wheels—was specially imported from England and donated by the locally owned insurance company. The firm also provided money to construct a water tank or reservoir for better fire protection.

During the 1860s, as more insurance businesses began operating in Halifax, the company expanded outside the city. By 1888 Halifax Fire Insurance had nine agencies in Nova Scotia and was helping to improve fire-fighting equipment in provincial towns. For the next thirty years the Halifax-based firm was a prosperous local business. Major losses were few. The most noteworthy exception came during the explosion of 1917. Fortunately most of the firm's resulting claim payments were recovered from the

provincial government the following year.

Nationwide expansion during the 1920s saw the company open successive branches in Quebec, Ontario, British Columbia, the Prairie provinces, and New Brunswick. In 1928 Halifax Fire Insurance extended its business into the United States and, later, farther abroad. As the concern expanded its geographical operations, it also offered different kinds of insurance. The corporate name was changed to The Halifax Insurance Company in 1939 to reflect its broader business.

Following World War II, Halifax Insurance was reorganized to cope

A notice dated March 28, 1809, to the members of the Fire Insurance Association.

with the changing insurance needs of Canadians. In Halifax, the firm opened a new headquarters on Spring Garden Road and Brenton Street in 1953. To mark the occasion, the original documents of

Halifax Fire Insurance went on public display in the new building. The firm, which began the same year King George III celebrated the Golden Jubilee of his reign, proudly pointed out it had served Canadians during the rule of nine English monarchs. "We are the only survivor of all the financial institutions that existed in Nova Scotia 144 years ago," noted an ad-

This policy was for fire insurance on the residence of Mr. Hugh Bell, a Methodist minister, and took effect January 1, 1816.

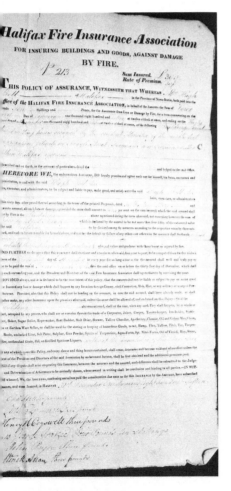

vertisement in 1953.

A year later Halifax Insurance ended its operations in the United States and concentrated on Canadian business. The company introduced new insurance plans to

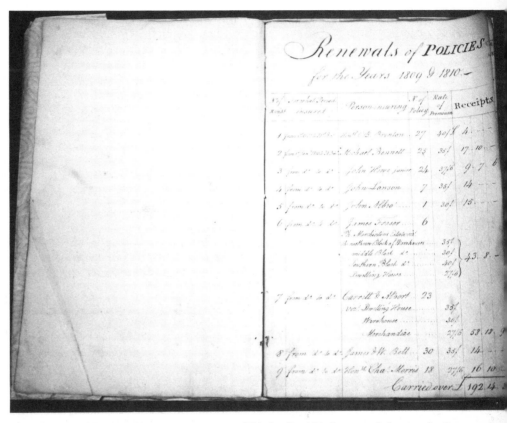

This fragile old ledger recorded renewals of policies for the years 1809 and 1810.

cover rental properties damage and family medical costs. Halifax Insurance also pioneered the use of one-page summaries on individual policies to make coverage terms more easily understood by customers.

On its 150th anniversary in 1959, Halifax Insurance was taken over by the Netherlands Insurance Company, established in 1845, which also controlled other insurance companies in Canada. These operations eventually merged and, under its new ownership, Halifax Insurance reasserted itself in Canada. From 1955 to 1972 the earned premiums of the firm increased from $3.7 million to more than $13 million. Part of that growth was visible in central Halifax. In 1965 Halifax Insurance moved into the ten-storey Halifax Insurance building. The $2.5-million office now houses the organization's Maritime branch.

By 1974 Halifax Insurance operated one of the industry's most advanced computerized systems for residential and car insurance. The firm was among the first to introduce home insurance that automatically adjusted the policy's value to inflation. Another innovation was providing special insurance for condominium owners.

The Halifax Insurance Company presently operates a dozen offices and branches across Canada from its general office in Toronto. Corporate assets reached $127 million in 1983. That year, Halifax Insurance proudly published its 175th annual report, complete with a map of nineteenth-century Nova Scotia on the front cover and a specially written story tracing the firm's growth since its founding in Halifax in 1809.

HALIFAX UNIVERSITIES

While serving as Atlantic Canada's centre of commerce, Halifax is also the heart of higher education for the region. Statesmen, scientists, surgeons, even space travellers have passed through the city's college corridors during the past two centuries. Today about 20,000 people are enrolled annually at Halifax's major degree-granting institutions, taking courses ranging from art design and astronomy to urban planning and women's studies. The concentration and variety of educational facilities in metro Halifax makes the city one of Canada's leaders in learning and research.

Dalhousie University is Halifax's largest, with more than 10,000 students, 3,000 courses, and 66 different buildings centred in the city's south end. From Dal's ranks have come prime ministers, Supreme Court justices, and provincial premiers, as well as leaders in business, science, and the arts. Begun in 1819 by the Earl of Dalhousie, then lieutenant-governor of Nova Scotia, the first Dalhousie College was a two-storey stone building on Halifax's Grand Parade, where city hall now stands. To finance the college, the lieutenant-governor used 11,000 pounds in customs duties collected by British troops while they occupied a seaport in Maine during the War of 1812.

The Earl of Dalhousie wanted the college in Halifax to be like the university in his Scottish home of Edinburgh and welcome students and staff of all religions. Such an attitude was ahead of its time and nearly doomed Dalhousie before a single degree was conferred. After the Earl left Halifax for higher colonial postings, the college became "swaddled in conflict and confusion," according to one historical account. Without its

influential founder, the idea of a non-denominational school gained little local support. Some teaching was done, but for many years Dalhousie remained disorganized and largely dormant.

In that era of British North America, education remained closely linked to the church. Such was the case of Halifax's first college, Saint Mary's University, established by the Reverend Edmund Burke in 1802 as a Catholic college for men. One of Canada's oldest universities, Saint Mary's first opened at the corner of Barrington Street and Spring Garden Road, financed entirely by Roman Catholic residents in Halifax. By 1841 Saint Mary's moved to nearby Grafton Street and became a chartered university, granting de-

Dalhousie University is Halifax's largest with more than 10,000 students, 3,000 courses, and 66 different buildings centred in the city's south end.

A view of the arts and administration building at Dalhousie University.

Dalhousie moved from its downtown building to the Halifax south end, into the red-brick Forrest Building, named after John Forrest, Dal's then-president. The college would later expand westward during the early 1900s, opening more classrooms, libraries, and the faculties of arts and science, and dentistry.

Marking Queen Victoria's Golden Jubilee in 1887, the Victoria School of Art opened on Halifax's Hollis Street, across from Province House. Among the founders was teacher Anna Leonowens, the heroine in the story *Anna and the King of Siam* (which inspired the popular musical, *The King and I*). The art school moved to George and Argyle streets, opposite the Grand Parade by 1909. This new home was actually the old National School, erected in 1818. That three-storey wooden structure, now used as a restaurant, remains the oldest school building in Halifax. The art school was incorporated in 1925 and renamed the Nova Scotia College of Art.

A different type of training in Halifax became available in 1909, when the Technical University of Nova Scotia opened its brick and stone building on Spring Garden Road. Originally known as the Technical College of Nova Scotia, it was founded to give centralized education in civil, electrical, mining, and mechanical engineering. Such technical training was offered to students after they completed general courses at other provincial colleges.

Saint Mary's College resumed post-secondary courses in 1913 at its newly acquired campus on Windsor Street, near Quinpool Road. In addition to its arts and

grees to students regardless of religion but remaining controlled by the Catholic Church.

Like Dalhousie, Saint Mary's also faced early problems. Both colleges were reorganized in the 1860s—Dal got an independent board of governors and began to grow, while Saint Mary's was transplanted to a site on Agricola Street. More changes came during the next decade, when the Nova Scotia government amalgamated Dalhousie, Saint Mary's, and the other colleges in the province as the University of Halifax. The arrangement proved short-lived. By 1881 the provincial government withdrew both its plan and its money. Saint Mary's, left without adequate financing, was forced to suspend teaching for some two decades, until a local benefactor helped revive the college with a

bequest of land and money.

In the meantime, the outskirts of Halifax became home for a learning academy exclusively for women. Located by Bedford Basin, the school was founded in 1873 by the Sisters of Charity of Saint Vincent de Paul, a teaching order of nuns. This ladies' academy grew to become Mount Saint Vincent University, the first independent college for women in Canada and the British Commonwealth. Mount Saint Vincent would go on to grant degrees to women in arts, science, home economics, library science, and education.

For Dalhousie College, the 1880s were years of expansion. Already boasting separate faculties of medicine and science, in 1883 Dal began its own law school, the first in the British Empire to give courses in common law. Four years later

science programs, Saint Mary's offered courses in engineering (in association with the Technical College of Nova Scotia) and commerce. Saint Mary's remained small. Annual convocations involved about thirty graduates. But, foreseeing a need for future growth, the college purchased the thirty-acre Gorsebrook golf course in 1943 for a new campus. Saint Mary's moved there in 1951, became officially known as Saint Mary's University the next year, and had more than 300 students enrolled by 1956.

The newest post-secondary school in Halifax is also Nova Scotia's oldest. The University of King's College was 134 years old when it became associated with Dalhousie in 1923. King's College was founded by United Empire Loyalists at Windsor, Nova Scotia, in 1789. Thirteen years later King George III granted the college its royal charter "for the education and instruction of youth and students in arts and faculties." King's College continued in the town of Windsor, fifty miles northwest of Halifax, until fire destroyed the main building in 1920. After the disaster, King's moved to Halifax and set up joint campus and teaching facilities with Dalhousie. Now with about 350 students, King's continues as a small, residential, and independent liberal arts college, modelled on the English universities of Oxford and Cambridge.

Contrasting such traditions, the Technical University of Nova Sco-

Saint Mary's University, shown here in the early 1950s, was established in 1802 and was Halifax's first college.

tia continues to aim for new ways to teach and use science. During World War II TUNS worked with the Nova Scotia Light and Power Company on a top-secret project for the Canadian Navy. The three partners successfully discovered how to use electricity to protect ships against German magnetic mines.

After the war TUNS began training increasing numbers of engineers in Nova Scotia. By 1962 the university had granted engineering degrees to more than 2,300 students. That decade also saw TUNS establish the first school of architecture in the Atlantic provinces as well as its own school of graduate studies and a computer centre. More laboratories, classrooms, offices, and a residence

Technical University of Nova Scotia's fourteen-acre campus is in downtown Halifax, a stone's throw from the harbour front and adjacent to the central business and commercial community. From left to right, examining the layout for the university's future, are Dr. L.F. Kirkpatrick, a member of the board of governors; Dr. J. Clair Callaghan, president of TUNS; and Dr. C.G. "Geoff" Meyerhof, professor emeritus.

were built on its growing downtown campus. TUNS even received a royal coat of arms. Graduate and post-graduate programs were added until present enrolment stands at about 1,000. Practical research is currently ongoing in a wide range of subjects—from fisheries technology and energy studies

Nova Scotia industry leader Dr. John Jodrey is chancellor of the Technical University of Nova Scotia. Dr. Jodrey is pictured at right as Dr. J. Clair Callaghan, president of TUNS, adjusts the robes of the chancellor's office.

to microcomputer design and offshore energy engineering.

Halifax's older schools grew as well. Mount Saint Vincent, rebuilt after a 1951 fire destroyed the original building, now has a total enrolment of about 2,300. The Mount began accepting male students in 1970, but the university's

Convocation at TUNS is a major interface with the community. Shown here is a view of the impressive scene at the 1985 convocation in the 10,000-seat Metro Centre in downtown Halifax.

primary aim remains providing higher education to women. Professional courses—including business administration, secretarial arts, and public relations—are offered in addition to arts programs.

The Nova Scotia College of Art moved into the St. Andrew's Presbyterian Church Hall on Coburg Road in 1957. The college's staff then numbered fewer than 10 and taught fewer than 100 students. Programs in commercial art, art education, and design were added and despite a major expansion of the former church hall in 1968, the art college again needed more space. After adopting a new name, the Nova Scotia College of Art and Design moved back downtown into the renovated historic buildings along the Granville Mall. The renovation and relocation took six years and put the art college two blocks from its original home. Today with 500 students and about 100 faculty, NSCAD is Canada's only degree-granting college of art and design.

Saint Mary's University now includes a dozen modern buildings in which to house and instruct its

5,000 full- and part-time students. Undergraduate degrees are offered in arts, science, and commerce as well as pre-professional programs. The Saint Mary's campus also features an observatory with Eastern Canada's most powerful reflecting telescope, a research institute for Atlantic Canada studies, and an international education centre.

Dalhousie University has grown with its faculties of graduate studies, health professions, and management studies. Self-contained in a two-storey building 150 years old, Dal's campus is now spread across sixty-seven acres of ivy-covered stone buildings, modern concrete complexes such as the Arts Centre and Killam Library,

plus frame homes converted into department offices.

Halifax's universities are now working co-operatively to share existing academic resources and develop new courses. The aim is for excellence in each academic program, wherever it's offered in metro. That commitment means the law school that attracted Prime Minister Brian Mulroney, the technical university that honoured astronaut Marc Garneau, and the other degree-granting institutions in Halifax will continue at Canada's education forefront.

Saint Mary's University now includes many modern buildings in which to house and instruct its 5,000 full- and part-time students.

HOYT'S MOVING AND STORAGE LTD.

Leonard Hoyt was thirteen years old when he got his start in the moving profession. In 1924 he helped move his family's farm machinery from the Minas Basin area to Truro, a distance of about twenty-five miles. That first experience turned into a career some six years later when his brother established Nova Scotia's first highway trucking company. The business, Hoyt's Transfer, was based in their hometown of Truro and operated routes connecting Halifax, Sydney, and Moncton, New Brunswick. Leonard Hoyt, nicknamed Benny, came to Halifax to manage the firm's local office. By 1935 Leonard, who maintained that his only hobby was his work, handled the regular freight shipments in Halifax and also began using the trucks to move furniture in the

This 1950 photograph shows the first office of Hoyt's Moving and Storage Ltd. on Young Street. After the firm moved to a larger facility outside the city in 1981, this building was used as a warehouse.

area. That secondary work was the start of what is now Atlantic Canada's largest moving and storage company.

When the partnership between the Hoyt brothers broke up in 1939, Leonard decided to stay in Halifax, running his moving business while his brother in Truro continued the highway transport company. By the following year Leonard Hoyt the Mover, the firm's original name, had become a well-known enterprise in Halifax. At first Hoyt used two small trucks, working out of a 2,000-square-foot

warehouse-garage in the city's north end. His business with both residential and commercial clients grew and the company was incorporated as Hoyt's Moving and Storage Ltd. in 1949. The headquarters on Young Street expanded many times over the years to keep up with the increasing volume of packing, storage, crating, and moving done by his business. By 1950 Hoyt's oversaw a fleet of eight highway transport trucks as well as smaller vehicles used for local jobs. Two years later the concern landed what was then its biggest job—moving a customer from the Atlantic coast to the Pacific. Hoyt's employee Lloyd Stewart became the first moving van driver to complete a sea-to-sea round trip in Canada, travelling 10,000 miles from Halifax to Victoria, British

Leonard Hoyt, founder.

Clifford Hoyt, president.

Columbia, and back.

Founder Leonard Hoyt continued as president until his death in 1961. Succeeding him was his eldest son, Clifford Hoyt. The moving company remained primarily a Halifax-Dartmouth operation until 1971. That year Hoyt's began expanding and quickly opened or acquired branch offices in Fredericton, Saint John, and Newcastle, New Brunswick. Hoyt's established another office in Middleton, Nova Scotia, in 1978. New warehouses were built in all these locations and the firm increased the number of vans in its fleet. By the 1980s Hoyt's operated more than 100 vans and trucks for local and long-distance moving. The firm is no longer confined to North American destinations as overseas moving jobs are also handled.

Another factor in Hoyt's success is its affiliation with United Van Lines. United is a national organi-

zation owned by independent moving companies throughout Canada. Thanks in part to Hoyt's participation, United Van Lines is the largest such organization in Canada. Clifford Hoyt, who is also a director and former president of United, says such a link gives his organization two advantages—allowing personal attention to local business while benefitting from nationwide purchasing, co-ordination, and advertising. Through its various regional operations, Hoyt's owns and operates twelve United Van Lines franchises in the Maritimes.

In 1978 Hoyt's pioneered using weatherized containers for moving household furniture in the region. These large, sanitized boxes are a faster and more convenient way to handle loads of furniture. Containers full of furnishings can be loaded from one vehicle to another, making transporting easier and safer since no repacking is required. Items can also be stored in these containers, further reducing handling and costs.

By 1981 Hoyt's original Halifax site on Young Street had grown into a 60,000-square-foot warehouse that covered six city building lots. But the location was no longer large enough for the firm's business. A few months prior to its forty-second anniversary, the company moved to a seven-acre property just outside the city of Halifax. The three major buildings on the site were custom-designed for Hoyt's and house its head office, warehouse, and vehicle garage. The Young Street property in Halifax is still used by Hoyt's for commercial storage space.

The moving company has a longtime involvement throughout the region as a corporate supporter of minor baseball and hockey teams. Perhaps Hoyt's most re-

markable example of community assistance came in February 1970, after the Liberian tanker *Arrow* spilled 1.5 million gallons of thick heating oil in Chedabucto Bay, near the Canso Strait. Some of the company's Halifax-based equipment was used to haul 13,000 bales of straw needed to contain the pollution in the affected areas. In three days Hoyt's staff and vehicles helped haul 500,000 pounds of straw from Nova Scotia's Annapolis Valley and neighbouring New Brunswick to aid the emergency clean-up.

President Clifford Hoyt is proud of the firm's commitment to the Maritimes. Hoyt's Moving and Storage Ltd. is still owned and operated by the founding family and a third generation—the grandchildren of founder Leonard Hoyt—are among the current staff of 200 permanent and part-time employees.

PAT KING GROUP LTD.

In 1951 Patrick King ran a one-man insurance agency from a rented office above the Dartmouth five-cents-to-a-dollar store. Today he oversees a multimillion-dollar business that employs more than 300 Atlantic Canadians in real estate, insurance, and affiliated companies. As chairman of Pat King Group Ltd., the English-born businessman is proud of the personal service his companies have maintained. "I'm doing business today with the sons and daughters of some of my original clients," he says.

Pat King first came to Dartmouth during World War II, serving on North Atlantic convoy patrols with the Royal Navy. In 1947 he settled in the town and began selling insurance from his home, developing a large clientele among local Navy personnel. When some of his sailor policyholders were transferred from Dartmouth, many asked Pat King to rent or sell their homes. Recognizing the opportunity, Pat King started a local real estate business in 1952, headquartered in a five-cents-to-a-dollar store on Portland Street. During the 1950s, while the number of Dartmouth property sales totalled just 200 a year (today's annual figure is about 1,200), Pat King's new realty business grew

The Pat King Group's headquarters at 52 Queen Street was completely renovated in the late 1960s. The mansard-style building became the symbol of the company.

and his insurance practice prospered.

In the 1960s his companies turned to land development, residential construction, and property appraisals in both Dartmouth and Halifax. As Pat King's real estate business increased, the firm modernized its Queen Street headquarters, completely renovating the exterior with a distinctive mansard roof. That steep-roofed style soon became the company's symbol. The first branch office of Pat King Real Estate opened in Halifax in 1969. In 1980 the administrative headquarters moved to its present premises on Main Street. By 1984 Pat King Real Estate operated nineteen offices in the province, four more in Newfoundland and Prince Edward Island, and was the leading realtor in Halifax-Dartmouth and Nova Scotia.

Much of the company's recent success is due to computer technology. In 1981 Pat King Real Estate was among the first realtors in Canada to computerize property listings and sales figures. With the touch of a button, its sales agents can find properties according to price, location, size, and features, making the job of matching home buyers and sellers vastly more efficient.

Pat King's involvement in community affairs has included his election as town alderman in 1960 and service as deputy mayor the following year, when Dartmouth became a city. He has also been appointed twice as president of the Halifax-Dartmouth Real Estate Board.

Pat King sits at one of the computer terminals used by his real estate company. The use of computers has revolutionized the real estate business in Atlantic Canada.

OLAND BREWERIES LIMITED

"As long as the grain ripens and the barley grows, people will drink beer."

—*Joe Howe,*
Nova Scotian statesman

Susannah Oland took Howe's words to heart when she first brewed her family's famous Brown October Ale more than a century ago. The beer this mother of seven made at her Dartmouth home began a family empire. In October 1867 Susannah and her husband founded the Army and Navy Brewery to sell their beer commercially. The original brewery was built on twelve acres of land near the site of the present Angus L. MacDonald Bridge. Susannah Oland was the first brewmistress, and she passed her skills to three of her sons. Following her husband's tragic death in 1870, Susannah and the rest of the family carried on the brewing business, later renaming it S. Oland Sons and Company in 1877.

The family continued their business despite two disastrous brewery fires during the next twenty years. A new brewery was built in Turtle Grove, Dartmouth (near the generating station). Upon Susannah's death in 1886, her sons took over until control was sold to English investors nine years later. Sons George and John maintained an investment in this new company. In 1905 George and his son, Sidney Oland, bought a Halifax brewery on Agricola Street and renamed it Oland & Son Ltd. John Oland was appointed brewmaster. That lasted until 1917, when the explosion levelled their brewery in Halifax and the brewery at Turtle

Oland's fleet of highway trucks uses state-of-the-art reflectorized tape for improved visibility at night.

Grove in Dartmouth, killing Susannah's son, Conrad. To continue market supply, George Oland bought the Simeon Jones Brewery (formerly the Red Ball Brewery) in Saint John, New Brunswick.

Colonel Sidney Oland rebuilt the Agricola Street brewery, which reopened in 1922. While those were Prohibition days, beer with about half the usual alcohol content could still be sold. The Oland business grew and in 1927 the firm purchased the then-century-old Alexander Keith Brewery on Halifax's Water Street. When Prohibition ended in Nova Scotia in 1930, Oland & Son Ltd. operated two thriving breweries in Halifax and one in Saint John.

With a white marble mansion in the city's south end and downtown business headquarters in elegant Keith Hall, the Olands were among Halifax's most prominent families. In 1963 the Olands commissioned construction of the *Bluenose II,* the full-size replica of Nova Scotia's famous schooner. Susannah's great-grandson, Victor B. Oland, became Nova Scotia's lieutenant-governor in 1968.

The Halifax-based Oland & Son Ltd. was merged with John Labatt Limited in 1971 and continues as

Oland Breweries Limited's Agricola Street brewery was purchased by the family in 1905. © Coldwell Photography

the best-selling brewery in the Maritimes. Oland Breweries Limited now brews such local beers as Schooner, Oland Export, Old Scotia Ale, Oland's Light Beer, and Keith's I.P.A. The Halifax brewery, which has remained on Agricola Street since 1922, now employs about 200 and recently underwent a $16-million renovation.

N.S. TRACTORS & EQUIPMENT LTD.

N.S. Tractors & Equipment Ltd. has sold and serviced heavy machinery throughout Atlantic Canada for more than half a century. The company started in 1927 as the construction machinery division of William Stairs, Son, and Morrow Ltd., a hardware firm that began in 1810 on Halifax's Lower Water Street. The Stairs' heavy machinery subsidiary was renamed N.S. Tractors & Equipment in 1959, five years after the present Kempt Road headquarters was built.

Since 1971 the concern has been independently owned and operated by Jack Craig, president, and Dean Trimper, vice-president, who expanded the number of products and services available. As exclusive

Jack Craig, president.

dealer in Nova Scotia for the Caterpillar brand of heavy equipment, the company supplies bulldozers, excavators, trucks, loaders, and much more. Whenever major construction or maintenance work is done in the area—a new building or an improved road, removing snow or installing bigger water mains—chances are the private contractor or local government crews are using machinery from N.S. Tractors & Equipment.

Not all of the firm's work is done at city construction sites. Generations of miners and foresters throughout the region have relied on N.S. Tractors for the large vehicles needed to move such products as coal, salt, or pulpwood. To transport manufactured goods, ranging from bottled beer to crated furniture, N.S. Tractors can provide compact electric-, gasoline-, propane-, and diesel-powered forklifts up to large container handlers. Such wide-ranging applications show the versatility of the company's lines of wheeled and truck-equipped products.

Recognizing the growing popularity of Caterpillar engines for other commercial uses, N.S. Tractors created its Industrial and Marine Power Division in 1981.

N.S. Tractors & Equipment Ltd. is the exclusive dealer in Nova Scotia for the Caterpillar brand of heavy equipment.

Diesel-fueled electrical power units are available from the firm for both temporary and permanent applications. In an emergency blackout, the Victoria General Hospital in Halifax would rely on a power generation plant supplied by N.S. Tractors. The company also installed backup power equip-

Dean Trimper, vice-president.

In the summer of 1984 the Bluenose II *led a parade of sailing vessels in the tall ships event in Halifax Harbour. The ship is equipped with Caterpillar 3304 generators and propulsion engines supplied by N.S. Tractors & Equipment Ltd.*

oil samples give a good picture of the engine and related components, which can provide indications of possible future problems. For example, excessive fuel, dirt, or microscopic pieces of metal found in equipment oil could be an early indication of future failure of

Streetcars were stalled for twelve hours by a snowstorm in February 1942. Caterpillar tractors removed snow and ice from streets in downtown Halifax.

ment for the newspaper presses and offices of the Halifax Herald Ltd. Recent construction projects in metro using auxiliary generators supplied by N.S. Tractors include the World Trade and Convention Centre, the Purdy's Wharf project, and Central Trust Tower.

Nova Scotia's world-famous sailing ambassador, the *Bluenose II,* is another customer of N.S. Tractors. During a 1984 refit, the two-masted schooner was equipped with a pair of Caterpillar auxiliary generators as well as switch gear custom-made by the Industrial and Marine Power Division. When the wind is too light to fill her canvas sails, the *Bluenose II* obtains power from two Caterpillar propulsion engines located below deck. N.S. Tractors supplies marine engines rated up to 6,000 horsepower for many other applications on ocean-going vessels, ranging from bow-thrusters for offshore supply ships to main engines for harbour tugs.

Customer service is another important aspect of N.S. Tractors. More than 24,000 kinds of spare parts, worth over several million dollars, are kept in stock at the

company's operations in Halifax, Sydney, and Yarmouth. N.S. Tractors is also linked to a continent-wide computer network throughout North America that quickly locates and orders less frequently needed parts and equipment for local customers.

Teams of service crews can quickly travel to any job site in the province or offshore where repairs are needed. To prevent unscheduled downtime, N.S. Tractors' personnel use sophisticated equipment to detect developing mechanical problems before major repairs are necessary. One method of equipment analysis pioneered in Nova Scotia by the firm is called Scheduled Oil Sampling. Under this program, oil from engines, transmissions, and hydraulic equipment is regularly tested by company technicians. The types and amounts of impurities in these

vital moving parts.

One of N.S. Tractors' largest customers in this program is the Metropolitan Transit Commission, the municipal bus agency in metro Halifax. Since 1978 Metro Transit's fleet of some 145 diesel buses is regularly given this preventive maintenance service. Acting as an early warning system, N.S. Tractors' program detects potential engine problems before major breakdowns occur. Thanks to N.S. Tractors' unique oil analysis, the lower bus repair bills at Metro Transit benefit taxpayers throughout the area.

In addition to the traditional Caterpillar line of heavy equipment, N.S. Tractors & Equipment Ltd. also sells hydraulic cranes, backhoe loaders, articulated dump trucks, plus Caterpillar and other branded backhoe loaders, and paving machinery.

203

IMPERIAL OIL LTD.

Canada's largest oil company became firmly established in Halifax in 1898, when Imperial Oil Ltd. joined forces with Frank and Sid Shatford, two brothers who in 1865 started Nova Scotia's first oil business. The Shatford boys (Sid was twenty, Frank, eighteen) began selling imported oil to local merchants after they saw American traders sail into Halifax with barrels of oil and quickly sail away with pockets full of money. "Life in the oil business was not all pleasure and glory," Sid Shatford wrote in 1954, recalling the early days. "However, we continued and we succeeded. . . . Business responded to our efforts and the oil business of Nova Scotia, which formerly was done in Boston, was diverted to Halifax."

In the late 1800s oil reached the East Coast by rail or in forty-gallon wooden barrels carried by ship. Using such carriers, Shatford Brothers Ltd., later renamed Eastern Oil Company, built a sales network extending throughout Nova Scotia, Prince Edward Island, and the colony of Newfoundland. For more than a decade the Shatfords competed with Imperial Oil. Then the rival concerns merged under the Imperial Oil name with Frank and Sid overseeing regional business. Shatford continued working for Imperial for the next forty-four years.

After the merger, Imperial built a million-gallon oil storage tank at Africville, in the Halifax north end, ensuring constant supplies for the Atlantic area. In 1910 the local Imperial Oil office had a staff of eleven serving 7,000 customers. Among the clients was the Halifax Electric Tramway Company, for which Imperial concocted a special lubricating oil to silence squealing tramcar wheels.

With the start of World War I,

Sidney Shatford was nineteen when this photo was taken in 1864. The following year he and his younger brother, Frank, started the Shatford Brothers Ltd. oil business in Halifax. Their company became part of Imperial Oil Ltd. in 1886.

demand for petroleum products rose dramatically in the region and Imperial decided to build a local oil refinery, the first in Atlantic Canada. The firm originally wanted the plant built at its north end property but Halifax officials, concerned about fire risks, blocked that plan. Imperial then bought 500 acres of farmland at Imperoyal, Woodside, three miles from the town of Dartmouth. When construction of the refinery began in 1916, the area was so isolated that many of the 1,500 workers lived in the company's on-site construction camp.

The Halifax explosion of December 1917 left workers and the unfinished refinery unscathed. But Imperial's crews and construction materials were rushed into Halifax to help survivors and to build emergency shelters. About 160 Haligonians left injured or homeless by the blast were housed, fed, and cared for at Imperial's Imperoyal, Woodside, camp.

When the refinery opened two months later, much of its 2,200-barrel daily production went toward wartime supplies. During the 1920s and 1930s demand for refined oil products continued to increase in Atlantic Canada. Airplanes became a glamorous market for oil products, and the nearby Shearwater air base provided Imperial with many high-flying customers. Amelia Earhart refuelled at the Imperoyal, Woodside, refinery in 1928 on her first transatlan-

tic flight. Charles and Anne Lindbergh also refuelled there as part of their Atlantic survey flights in 1933. Today the company continues to supply aviation products to private, commercial, and military aircraft.

During World War II the refinery was an important fuel depot for the Allies. The facility was expanded and supplied twenty-five million barrels of bunker fuel for 10,500 warships, convoy-bound freighters, and troop carriers (including the *Queen Elizabeth*). Imperial's refinery was also part of Operation Shuttle—processing the oil later shipped secretly across the Atlantic.

By the early 1950s the refinery's daily capacity had increased more than tenfold since 1918, but still more oil products were needed. Imperial spent thirty million dollars in 1955-1956 to update and enlarge its plant. The job, which required 1,200 workers, was the

largest single refinery contract ever completed in Canada to that time. The newly expanded refinery, which processed crude oil shipped mainly from Venezuela, had a capacity of 45,000 barrels a day.

Constant improvements have continued at the refinery during the past thirty years to keep pace with changing technology and economics. Following the energy crisis of the 1970's, Imperial modified its only East Coast refinery to use crude oil from wells in Mexico, the Middle East, and the North Sea. As oil prices rose, so did the refinery's efficiency, while keeping high standards for environmental protection and employee safety. In 1984 a $100-million modernization program was under way at the 66-year-old refinery. At the touch of a button a new computer system can blend gasoline or keep track of oil volumes. That's a blessing for the refinery's 340-member work force since the plant can process more

Imperial Oil's Dartmouth Refinery was ten years old when this photograph was taken in 1928.

than 84,000 barrels of oil a day, yield forty-two different petroleum-based products, and annually produce about 4.5 billion litres of gasoline, heating oil, and other fuels.

Imperial Oil's presence in metro Halifax isn't limited to its refinery. The company was among the pioneers in East Coast offshore exploration during the 1970s. From its Atlantic Region office in Scotia Square, Imperial oversees the more than twenty-five Esso service stations in metro, a network of home-heating centres, and a seven-vessel marine division based in Dartmouth. On behalf of its 14,700 employees in Canada, including 551 in metro, Imperial Oil Ltd. is a major corporate sponsor of many local sports, community, and cultural activities.

NOVA SCOTIA SAVINGS & LOAN COMPANY

"There's a special kind of relationship between a local financial institution and the public," says James E. Radford, president of Nova Scotia Savings & Loan, a company that has handled money for Haligonians for more than 135 years. Nova Scotia Savings is the oldest financial firm of its kind in Canada and now does business throughout the country. From the organization's head office, which has remained in Halifax since the company began operating on August 5, 1850, Radford is proud of both the history and the future of Nova Scotia Savings & Loan. "We're building on a long, strong past," he says, "and are looking forward to continued expansion as well as adding new financial services."

The company started as a cooperative saving and lending institution named Nova Scotia Benefit Building Society and Savings Fund. The idea for such building societies came from Britain as a way people could pool their money into a fund from which prospective home owners obtained mortgage loans. The mortgages were then repaid over time, making homes affordable to those who lacked a large amount of cash yet had a steady income. The mortgage repayments and interest, plus continuing deposits by society members, kept the fund increasing in value.

In 1849 Nova Scotia politicians found that such building societies "enable persons of little or no capital to become owners of real estate on easy terms" and permitted such groups to operate. The Halifax-based organization was the third such group formed in British North America and proved popular and successful. By 1851, 201 Haligonians and Dartmouthians were investing or borrowing money through the society. Assets at the end of that first year totalled the equivalent of $22,000.

Initially the society arranged mortgages only on properties within three miles of Halifax's Market Square. The society's original directors—prominent businessmen, lawyers, and politicians—believed operating further afield was too risky. The first mortgage approved by the new Nova Scotia Benefit Building Society was for a three-storey frame house in Dartmouth. Both the mortgage and the building proved sound; in fact, the house remains standing along Dartmouth's busy Ochterloney Street.

From that start, the company quickly grew and was instrumental in financing much-needed housing in the Halifax area. By 1867 Nova Scotia Benefit Building Society's assets totalled more than half a million dollars. Five years later, as construction declined in Halifax, the firm expanded operations throughout Nova Scotia. By 1900 the company was represented by the more than a dozen agencies in Nova Scotia, from Yarmouth to North Sydney, plus another two in New Brunswick.

During this era Nova Scotia Benefit Building Society became one of the first businesses in Halifax to install typewriters and telephones. People came into the company's office just to see these then-novel inventions operating. The business changed its name in 1905 to the Nova Scotia Savings, Loan, and Building Society and its assets continued to grow. Despite two world wars and cycles of boom times and bad times, the firm continued to provide reliable and trusted financial services. By 1930 assets had reached $2.5 million. Between then and the outbreak of World War II, Nova Scotia Savings, Loan, and Building Society expanded more rapidly than in any earlier period. Assets increased to over four million dollars by 1940. To meet the increasing business from its more than 1,000 members, in 1938 the firm moved its head office in Halifax into larger quarters, the former Acadian Recorder building on Granville Street. By 1945 Nova Scotia Savings' assets rose to $5.3 million and staff at the new headquarters used the latest in office equipment, such as the first automatic bookkeeping machine in the province.

The postwar building boom saw the society offer 5 percent mortgages and both lending and savings activity reached new heights. At its centennial in 1950, the firm had assets of $8.9 million. Despite its growth in business, Nova Scotia Savings retained a family feeling among members, the majority of whom lived in Halifax County. By 1965 the society had financed more than 45,000 homes in the Halifax-Dartmouth area. That year the firm was reorganized and became Nova Scotia Savings & Loan (NSSL) Company. The change allowed more business outside the province and paved the way for even further expansion. Assets reached $38 million in 1966, the year NSSL moved south on Granville Street into its modern headquarters in Halifax's Centennial Building. Meanwhile, the company opened a branch in Dartmouth. NSSL then began financing apartment construction and lending to large institutions in other parts of Canada. By 1971 assets passed the $100-million mark and quadrupled during the next nine years.

In 1985 the company's 140-member staff operated twelve offices—six in Nova Scotia, including two in both Halifax and Dartmouth and one each in Truro and New

Glasgow; two in New Brunswick; and one each in Prince Edward Island, Newfoundland, Calgary, and Toronto.

This is the story of a unique Halifax company: Nova Scotia Benefit Building Society in 1850 to Nova Scotia Savings & Loan in 1985. It grew from $22,000 in assets to $.5 billion without losing, during those 135 years, its "family business" feeling. The firm started as a co-operative savings and lending institution, built on the integrity and industry of its members, and the preeminent role of Nova Scotia Savings' people is still true today. Dedicated, competent staff and management who have understood and managed change have been the traditional strengths since 1850.

Now NSSL is gearing up for another period of industry change.

James E. Radford, president of Nova Scotia Savings & Loan Company.

The recent installation of a new state-of-the-art computerized branch banking system, the launch of a new trust company subsidiary and a broadening of the range of financial services for personal and corporate customers continue a tradition of growing with the business.

AIR CANADA

A silver, twin-engine Trans-Canada Air Lines plane, piloted by Captain Walter Fowler, touched down at the old Eastern Passage airport on April 16, 1941, and brought with it a new era of travel to metro Halifax. TCA's Lockheed Super Electra "air ship," which landed at the RCAF airfield outside Dartmouth, was actually a day late. A Halifax-bound TCA plane had left Moncton, New Brunswick, the morning before, but fog at the Eastern Passage airport (now CFB Shearwater) prevented the aircraft from landing. After circling Halifax, the plane was forced back to Moncton. The fog cleared twenty-four hours later and a full plane-load of ten passengers, two pilots, and a stewardess landed at the

Staff members of TCA prepared to take off in a DC-3 on April 1, 1947, on a familiarization flight from Halifax to Boston.

Halifax Airport the next day on schedule at 8:49 a.m. "This is an historic event, one long awaited in this part of Canada," announced the *Halifax Mail* newspaper. "The publicly owned air service in this country is now Trans-Canada in fact as well as in name."

More than four decades since TCA's inaugural flight to Halifax, the airline's modern jets link Halifax directly to the United States, the United Kingdom, Bermuda, and major Canadian cities from coast to coast. A modern commercial airport on metro's outskirts now handles arrivals and departures of both passengers and cargo.

When Halifax International Airport opened in 1960, the pride of TCA's fleet was the Vickers Viscount, the world's first turbine-propeller airplane.

Flight tickets are no longer written by hand but issued by computer. Another change was in the TCA name, which became Air Canada in 1965 in recognition of the airline's growing worldwide presence. The corporation's fleet of 110 aircraft now regularly flies to sixty-three cities on three continents. Yet Air Canada's strong regional presence remains unchanged, says Bernie Miller, Air Canada's vice-president for Atlantic Canada and a native

Haligonian. "We pioneered commercial air transportation in Canada, and Halifax has developed into the hub of our Atlantic Canada network."

A recent example of Air Canada's commitment to metro is the airline's newly built cargo terminal at the Halifax Airport. Air Canada's freight shipments from Halifax have nearly tripled in the past decade and the new, $3.8-million cargo facility will help the airline handle even more freight. Also growing are the number of passengers flying on Air Canada from Halifax, with more than 400,000 people carried by the airline in 1983.

It's a far cry from April 1, 1940, when two Trans-Canada Air Lines employees, Stewart Sime and Paul Emmerson, set up the company's first Halifax ticket office in the lobby of the Nova Scotian Hotel.

Sod was turned in the summer of 1984 for Air Canada's multimillion-dollar cargo terminal at Halifax Airport. From left are Air Canada employees Sherry Feener and Wayne Blackburn and Bernie Miller, the firm's Atlantic Canada vice-president.

engine Douglas DC-3, which flew from Halifax to Yarmouth, Saint John, New Brunswick, then on to Boston. The same aircraft was used in 1948 on TCA's first non-stop Halifax to Montreal flights.

The late 1940s was an exciting time for air travel as more people took to the skies and Halifax became an important destination for transatlantic air traffic. Dignitaries and celebrities alike arrived in the city, often flying on TCA for the New York-Halifax leg of their journey. One popular young Hollywood movie star who arrived in Halifax then was Ronald Reagan.

By 1955 Halifax had become TCA's regional operations base and the company's main Halifax offices moved to Rainnie Drive. During the 1960s the airline's Halifax operations grew tremendously. On April 1, 1960, Transoceanic flights to Scotland and England commenced using Super Constellation aircraft. Another major change was the opening of the

At that time, TCA was three years old and operating just three aircraft across Canada. TCA's most eastern destination then was Moncton, so Halifax air passengers had to travel to that New Brunswick city before actually stepping on board a TCA plane. The delay in adding Halifax to TCA's regular schedule caused local concern but was mainly due to wartime shortages. When more planes and pilots became available, air service at Halifax increased to become, as a local newspaper observed, "more in keeping with (the city's) impor-

tance as a great Empire port and vital link in the future (of) air transport development."

In 1944 Trans-Canada Air Lines began a Halifax-Sydney route. Three years later the first regularly scheduled international flight from Halifax was started by TCA. Up to twenty-one passengers could travel in the airline's new, twin-

A gathering of past and present Air Canada staff in April 1976 marked the airline's thirty-fifth anniversary of service to Halifax. From left are Captain Walter Fowler, pilot of the first TCA flight to Halifax; Claude Taylor, Air Canada's current chairman; Stewart Sime, former district sales manager for TCA; and Paul Emmerson, one of TCA's first employees in Halifax.

During the late 1940s among the famous people who passed by the Halifax TCA office was Hollywood movie star Ronald Reagan, who later became the fortieth President of the United States.

Halifax International Airport on July 31, 1960. To maintain its flight schedules, TCA's Halifax staff had less than five hours one night to move from the Eastern Passage facility to the new airport thirty miles away. The transfer, which involved moving everything from wall clocks to loading ramps, went smoothly and the airline's Halifax personnel were ready to receive the first regularly scheduled arrival at the airport—an early-morning TCA flight from Montreal en route to St. John's, Newfoundland.

A new generation of jets touched

down in Halifax in 1961 when the first four-engine DC-8s were added to Halifax flight schedules. Later a $1.6-million maintenance base was built at the Halifax Airport and a new automated ticket reservation system was introduced. After the corporate name change to Air Canada, the airline added flights to destinations such as Bermuda and introduced the DC-9 aircraft to its Halifax runs.

Since then Air Canada has constantly been updating both its ground and air service. In 1976, the company's thirty-fifth anniversary of service into Halifax, Air Canada opened a crew base at the local airport. The next year the

Some of Air Canada's Atlantic regional staff in Halifax in 1985 included (top, left to right) Debbie Simon, Kim Burke, Mary MacIntosh, Mary Lamb, Ken Grant, and Gordie Lucas. In the bottom row are (left to right) David Pember, Peter McCarthy, Paul Machina, Michael Lezama, Bernard Miller, Nancy Fitzgerald, and Greg Corbett.

airline established an Atlantic regional office based in Halifax. At the same time Air Canada's downtown offices were consolidated at Scotia Square, where they remain today. Through its sponsorship of a wide variety of cultural, educational, and sporting events, Air Canada and its current metro Halifax staff of 500 plays an active role in the community. The airline is also proud of its assistance to charitable organizations and medical facilities throughout the Atlantic region.

Air Canada's latest aircraft, the Boeing 767, first arrived in Halifax in the spring of 1983. Compared to the TCA plane that landed in metro forty-one years earlier, this new wide-body aircraft can carry ten times as many passengers and travel twice as fast. Such advances in aviation are typical of Air Canada's goal of providing top-flight convenience to customers in Halifax and throughout the Atlantic provinces.

STANDARD PAVING MARITIME LIMITED

Until 1968 the Halifax head office of Standard Paving was on Lady Hammond Road, overlooking the Bedford Basin.

The streets in Halifax may not be paved with gold, but many have been paved by Standard Paving Maritime Limited, one of Atlantic Canada's oldest construction firms. "We've come a long way," says Richard Titus, president of the company since 1959. In those days, Titus recalls that completing 125 feet of concrete curbs and gutters was a good day's work. Today the company's modern machinery can do the same job more than ten times faster.

Standard Paving started in Halifax and opened its first office in July 1931 in the old Capitol Theatre building. A subsidiary of a Toronto-based construction company, Standard Paving quickly established a sound reputation in the area. "The improvements in the streets of this city by the laying of miles of new paving (by the company) is an effort that has been received with the endorsement of the citizens at large," wrote a Halifax newspaper in 1932. Among local projects Standard Paving completed in its first decade were surfacing such city streets as Almon, Barrington, and Gottingen, as well as covering the Bedford Highway with concrete pavement.

The company later moved its headquarters to Lady Hammond Road, then on the outskirts of Halifax. During the 1950s Stan-

dard Paving worked throughout the Maritime provinces on major road-building projects. Locally, the firm helped construct the Armdale Rotary and paved the approaches for the Angus L. MacDonald Bridge. Standard Paving has surfaced airport runways, ocean port terminals, parking lots, and private driveways. The company even installed the second rubberized running track in Canada, at Dalhousie

ten million dollars worth of equipment, including asphalt plants, crushers, pavers, and excavators. Such expansion recently allowed Standard Paving to undertake such major projects in Halifax as completing $9.5 million worth of street and sewer installations and $2.6 million of waterfront improvements.

The heavy construction company employs more than 400 seasonal workers, has an annual payroll exceeding $3.5 million, and has won numerous awards for job safety. Standard Paving president Titus is

Building the Angus L. MacDonald Bridge across Halifax Harbour during the early 1950s required workers and heavy equipment from Standard Paving.

University in 1966.

Two years later the Halifax-based venture relocated to its present site opposite Kearney Lake and continued to grow. Titus estimates the company now does ten times more work than twenty years ago. To keep up with demand, Standard Paving operates three branch offices and owns more than

well-known locally for his community work. He heads the Nova Scotia Oilers American Hockey League team and served as chairman of the Halifax Metro Centre and Halifax Forum Commission. Titus and Standard Paving vice-president J. Daniel Arbing are also active in the Nova Scotia Road Building Association.

ROYAL BANK OF CANADA

On May 2, 1864, seven prominent Haligonians opened their own banking house near the city's bustling waterfront. Originally called the Merchants Bank, the small firm started arranging loans and accepting deposits in a rented building on Bedford Row. From its Halifax birthplace, the business grew to become today's Royal Bank of Canada, the largest bank in the country and operating more than 1,750 branches throughout the world.

In the mid-nineteenth century Halifax was a good place to start a bank. The Nova Scotia capital was prospering as an international trading centre with six banks in the city. Although the boom times soon ended and the local economy slowed, the Merchants Bank remained profitable. During the bank's first five years of operation, its founders earned an average annual profit of 9 percent.

After Canada's Confederation in 1867, new banking laws were proposed that restricted the growth of privately owned banks. The Halifax-based banking house was reorganized, renamed the Merchants Bank of Halifax, and began a poli-

Rowland Frazee, chairman and chief executive officer.

cy of expansion that continues today. In 1869, the year the bank received full banking privileges from the newly formed Parliament of Canada, its assets amounted to $729,000.

The revamped Merchants Bank of Halifax soon began opening branches throughout Nova Scotia—in towns like Pictou and Sydney, Bridgewater, and Lunenberg. The Merchants Bank thrived and built a new Halifax headquarters at the corner of George and Hollis streets in 1879. Some ninety years later the bank—under its modern name—would open its thirteen-storey Royal Bank Tower on the same site.

Operations of the Merchants Bank increased during the 1880s. Five new branches opened in New Brunswick in 1882, the same year the company ventured into international banking with an office in Bermuda. But in 1885 two major Nova Scotia industries, both large borrowers from the Merchants Bank, went out of business. The bank suffered a loss that year, the only time in its history it failed to post an annual profit. However, the experience led to better lending policies and a renewed emphasis on expansion and diversification. Those decisions helped the institution become national in scope.

From Halifax, the Merchants Bank's operations grew in two directions—south along the traditional Maritime trade route to the Caribbean, and west following the new railroads into Central Canada and beyond. In 1899 the Merchants Bank operated forty-two branches, extending into Quebec, Ontario, British Columbia, New York City, and Havana, Cuba. By then two-thirds of the bank's

branches were outside Nova Scotia. To reflect its broader Canadian and international outlook, and to avoid confusion with two similarly named banks, the Merchants Bank adopted in 1901 a new name, the Royal Bank of Canada.

As the Royal's assets grew from twenty million dollars to fifty million dollars during the next six years, an increasing amount of business was conducted through Montreal, then Canada's largest city. Accordingly, the Royal's head office moved there from Halifax in 1907. Meanwhile, the bank continued to expand on all fronts. The Union Bank of Halifax was purchased in 1910, furthering the Royal's activity in both the Maritimes and the Caribbean. The bank's total number of branches increased to 207.

The Halifax explosion of December 1917 damaged the Royal's main downtown office, but the staff escaped with minor injuries,

The Royal Bank of Canada began in Halifax as the Merchants Bank, which was established in 1864. Its first office was in this rented building on Bedford Row.

This 1905 photograph shows the Royal Bank's Halifax office, located at the corner of George and Hollis streets.

The Royal Bank of Canada's Halifax main branch building as it appeared in the 1920s.

according to company records. A bank employee gave this eyewitness account: "Downstairs in Halifax Branch, the morning mail was spread out on the desks. . . . Suddenly the windows were demolished and with the ensuing backdraft the whole works was sucked out onto Hollis Street and the staff had to swarm out to the street to recover it." The Royal Bank of Canada was a major contributor to the Halifax Relief Fund, which aided victims of the explosion.

In the mid-1920s the Royal Bank acquired the Union Bank of Canada, which had 320 branches, 212 of them in the western provinces.

By 1929, following further expansion, the Royal was the largest bank in Canada, with assets exceeding one billion dollars. During the subsequent years of the Depression, followed by World War II, the Royal maintained and solidified its position as the country's leading banking institution. The Royal operated 727 branches in 1949, including sixty-two outside

Canada. Growth accelerated in the following decades, thanks to banking innovations the Royal helped introduce to Canadians, such as consumer credit cards and computerized banking systems.

During the 1960s the Royal was the first to build a modern high rise in the Halifax downtown core. The official opening of the Royal Bank Tower, on September 6, 1968, marked a new chapter in the development of both the bank and the city. The building houses the Royal's main Halifax branch, the bank's Atlantic regional headquarters, and an international banking centre. Currently about 800 people work at the Royal's twenty-four branches in metro Halifax. The bank, now the fourth-largest in North America, operates in forty-seven countries with total assets in 1983 worth more than eighty-four billion dollars.

Since 1980 the Royal Bank of Canada has been headed by Halifax-born Rowland Frazee, chairman and chief executive officer. The son of a bank manager, Mr. Frazee began his career with the Royal in New Brunswick when he was eighteen. After serving in World War II and later attending King's College and Dalhousie University, Mr. Frazee rejoined the bank. He has worked for the Royal Bank in a number of Canadian cities including Halifax, Winnipeg, Toronto, and Montreal. In addition to his business and community service work, Mr. Frazee holds honorary law degrees from four Maritime universities, including King's and Dalhousie.

The thirteen-storey Royal Bank Tower, the first high-rise office building in downtown Halifax, was opened in September 1968.

213

MOOSEHEAD BREWERIES LTD.

After a half-century of making beer for Maritimers, Canada's oldest independent brewery discovered a new market. In 1978 Moosehead Breweries Ltd. began shipping its beer south to the United States. Millions of cases later, the firm's aptly named Moosehead Canadian Lager Beer became the fourth-largest-selling imported beer in the United States. The privately owned brewery also made its mark overseas in 1980, when Moosehead's products captured five gold medals for brewing excellence at a world competition.

The firm attributes the wide popularity of its beers—like Alpine, Moosehead, and the recently reintroduced James Ready brand—to quality and innovation. The brewery was the first in Eastern Canada to sell beer in aluminum cans and, more recently, in custom-designed, long-necked bottles. With breweries in Dartmouth and Saint John, New Brunswick, Moosehead is also a major sponsor of sports throughout the region.

The company began in 1928 as an offshoot of the Oland family brewing business. The Olands started a home brewery in Dartmouth in 1867, which prospered until it was destroyed in the 1917 Halifax explosion. Two years later the family was back in the brewing business after buying a brewery in Saint John. Although Prohibition was then in force, beer containing little alcohol (called "near beer") could still be sold. Profits from the new Oland business helped the family build a new Halifax brewery in 1924. Three years later the Olands bought another beer-making company in Saint John, a brewery once run by local brew-

Moosehead Breweries Ltd. is located in Burnside Industrial Park in Dartmouth.

The ales and lagers brewed by Moosehead won five gold medals for quality at a world competition in 1980.

master James Ready. Known in 1928 as New Brunswick Breweries, it was the forerunner of today's Moosehead Breweries.

In the 1930s the various sons inherited stores in separate breweries and became business rivals. New Brunswick Breweries, although still owned by a branch of the Oland family, became a completely separate company from the brewery which retained the family name.

At first, New Brunswick Breweries made only one beer—James Ready's Ale. Later it introduced the Moosehead brand, then other beers like Ten-Penny and Alpine. With sales growing beyond its home province, New Brunswick Breweries changed its name to Moosehead Breweries in 1947.

The firm expanded in 1964 by opening a brewery at Dartmouth's Burnside Industrial Park. Ironically, the location is near the original Oland home site, where the family brewing tradition began more than a century ago. Currently more than 100 full-time staff members work in Dartmouth, including company president Derek Oland, grandson of Moosehead's founder.

The Moosehead family of beers became available in long-necked bottles throughout the Maritimes in 1984.

PATRONS

The following individuals, companies, and organizations have made a valuable commitment to the quality of this publication. Windsor Publications and the Halifax Board of Trade gratefully acknowledge their participation in *Halifax: Cornerstone of Canada.*

Acadian Lines Limited*
Air Canada*
Andres Wines Atlantic
Atlantic Photo Supply Ltd.
The Bank of Nova Scotia*
Alfred J. Bell and Grant Ltd.*
Ben's Ltd.*
Bonsai Shoppe Limited
Buckley's Drug Store
Budget Car and Truck Rentals
Burgess Transfer and Storage Ltd.
Canada Wire and Cable Ltd.
J.C. Esteves Cardoso
CBCL Limited
Central Trust Company*
Chandler, Moore
Creightons Limited
Jane Danielson
Doane Raymond*
Dover Mills Limited
Dumaresq & Bryne Ltd.-Architects
Billy & Andrew Duncan
The Edgecombe Group
Farmers Co-operative Dairy Limited*
The Friends of the Citadel Society
Halifax Cablevision Limited
Halifax Developments Limited*
The Halifax Herald*
Halifax Industries Limited*
The Halifax Insurance Company*
Halifax Port Corporation
Halifax Universities*
Hardy Freeman and Thomson Limited
Harris & Roome Ltd.
Heffler & Inkpen Insurance Services Ltd.
Historic Properties Limited
Hoyt's Moving and Storage Ltd.*
I.M.P. Group Limited*
Imperial Oil Ltd.*
Industrial Estates Limited
Johnson & Higgins Willis Farber Limited
Pat King Group Ltd.*
Lawson Graphics Atlantic
Library Department, Halifax District School Board
MacInnes Wilson Flinn Wickwire

Fred MacNeil
Maritime Flavour Gallery
The Maritime Life Assurance Company*
Maritime Paper Products Ltd.*
H.H. Marshall Limited*
I.H. Mathers & Son Limited*
Midland Doherty Limited
Moirs Division, Nabisco Brands Ltd.*
Montreal Trust*
Moosehead Breweries Ltd.*
Nova Scotia Power Corporation*
Nova Scotia Savings & Loan Company*
N.S. Tractors & Equipment Ltd.*
N.W. Atlantic Fisheries Organization
Oland Breweries Limited*
F.C. O'Neill, Scriven and Associates, Ltd.
Patterson Broadcasters Ltd.*
Payzant Building Products Ltd.
Price Waterhouse
Provincial Sanitary Products Ltd.
Public Service Commission of Halifax
Ramsen Engineering Associates Inc.
Reed Stenhouse Limited
Royal Bank of Canada*
Sable Gas Systems Limited
Scotia Bond Company Limited
Seaman Cross Limited*
Silver's Agencies Limited
Standard Paving Maritime Limited*
Stonehedge Developments Ltd.
Swift Eastern
Triton Engineering Limited
Twin City Management Limited
Volvo Canada Ltd.*
Westburne Industrial Enterprises Ltd.
Wood Motors Ford Limited*
Zellers Inc.

*Partners in Progress of *Halifax: Cornerstone of Canada.* The histories of these companies and organizations appear in Chapter 12, beginning on page 160.

BIBLIOGRAPHY

BOOKS, BOOKLETS, AND PAMPHLETS

Akins, Thomas Beamish. *History of Halifax City.* Belleville Ontario: Mika Publishing, 1973. (Original edition published Halifax: Nova Scotia Historical Society, 1895.)

Annand, William. *The Speeches and Public Letters of Joseph Howe.* Boston: John P. Jewett and Co., 1858.

Blakeley, Phyllis R. *Glimpses of Halifax, 1867-1900.* Halifax: Public Archives of Nova Scotia, 1949.

_____. *The Story of Nova Scotia.* Toronto: J.M. Dent & Sons (Canada) Limited, 1950.

Bourinot, Sir John G. *Builders of Nova Scotia.* Toronto: Copp-Clark Co. Ltd., 1900.

Bridgwater, William and Elizabeth Sherwood, eds. *The Columbia Encyclopedia.* New York: Columbia University Press, 1950.

Burbidge, Dean G.A. and Dr. M.D. Morrison. *Historical Sketches of St. Andrew's Church.* Halifax: 1949.

Campbell, Duncan. *Nova Scotia in its Historical, Mercantile and Industrial Relations.* Montreal: James Lovell, 1873.

Chambers, Robert W. *Halifax in Wartime, A Collection of Drawings.* Text by Frank W. Doyle. Halifax: *The Halifax Herald and the Halifax Mail,* 1943.

Churchill, Winston S. *The Second World War, Vol. IV: The Hinge of Fate.* Cambridge, MA: Houghton Mifflin Company, 1950.

_____. *The Second World War, Vol. V: Closing the Ring.* Canada: Thomas Allen Limited, 1951.

Connelly, Pearl. *The Bicentennial of the Halifax Fire Department, 1768-1968: 200 Years of Fire-Fighting.* Halifax: Pearl Connelly, 1968.

Dennis, Clara. *More About Nova Scotia.* Toronto: Ryerson Press, 1937.

Dyott, William. *Diary, 1781-1845.* Vol. I. Edited by Reginald W. Jeffrey. London: Archibald Constable & Co. Ltd., 1907.

Elliott, Shirley B. *A History of Province House.* Halifax: Nova Scotia Government Publication.

Fergusson, Bruce and William Pope. *Glimpses into Nova Scotia History.* Windsor, N.S.: Lancelot Press Ltd., 1974.

Founded Upon a Rock. 2nd ed. Halifax: Heritage Trust of Nova Scotia, 1971.

Giesler, Patricia. *Valour Remembered: Canadians in Korea.* Ottawa: Minister of Supply and Services, 1982.

Halifax, Nova Scotia and Its Attractions. Howard & Kutsche, circa 1900.

Hamilton, Dr. William B. *The Nova Scotia Traveller, A Maritimer's Guide to His Home Province.* Toronto: Macmillan of Canada, A Division of Gage Publishing Ltd., 1981.

Harris, Reginald V. *Catalogue of Portraits of the Judges of the Supreme Court of Nova Scotia and Other Portraits.* Halifax.

Harvey, D.C. *A View of Halifax, 1749-1949.* Proceedings of the Royal Society of Canada, Vol. XLIII, Series III. June 1949.

Hill, Kay. *Joe Howe, the Man Who Was Nova Scotia.* Toronto: McClelland and Stewart, 1980.

Kellock, Hon. Mr. Justice R.L. *Report on the Halifax Disorders.* Ottawa: King's Printer, 1945.

Kerr, D.G.G. *A Historical Atlas of Canada.* Toronto: Thomas Nelson & Sons (Canada) Ltd., 1959.

Lawson, Mrs. William. *History of the Townships of Dartmouth, Preston, and Lawrencetown.* Belleville, Ontario: Mika Studio, 1973. (Originally published in 1893 by Morton & Co, Halifax, N.S.)

McLeod, Robert R. *The History, Natural Resources and Native Beauties of Markland or Nova Scotia.* Toronto: Markland Publishing Company, 1903.

Marble, Allan. *Nova Scotians at Home and Abroad.* Windsor, N.S.: Lancelot Press, 1977.

Martell, James Stuart. *The Romance of Government House.* Revised ed. Halifax: Nova Scotia Communications and Information Centre, 1979.

Martin, John Patrick. *Historic Halifax, N.S. From the Citadel, A Pocket Guide Book.* Halifax: Tourist and Travel Dept. of the City of Halifax, 1949.

Martin, Dr. John Patrick. *The Story of Dartmouth.* Dartmouth, N.S.: Dr. John Patrick Martin, 1957.

Metson, Graham. *An East Coast Port . . . Halifax at War, 1939-1945.* Toronto: McGraw-Hill Ryerson, 1981.

Mullane, George. *Footprints Around and About Bedford Basin.* Halifax: Acadian Recorder.

Murdoch, Beamish. *A History of Nova Scotia or Acadie.* 3 vols. Halifax: Barnes, Printer and Publisher, 1867.

Nova Scotia Legislature, The. Halifax: Nova Scotia Communications and Information Centre, 1979.

Nova Scotia Magazine. December 1971. Halifax: Nova Scotia Government Publication, 1971.

Now it Can be Told, the Eastern Canadian Port. Halifax: Nova Scotia Light & Power Company Ltd., 1946.

Payzant, Joan and Lewis Payzant. *Like a Weaver's Shuttle, A History of the Halifax-Dartmouth Ferries.* Halifax: Nimbus, 1979.

Pullen, Rear Admiral Hugh F. *The Sea Road to Halifax.* Halifax:

From Dartmouth Hills at Twilight

A pale new moon—a slender silver sickle
Hangs hesitantly in the western sky.
Then slowly sinks behind the spires and turrets
Where churches, schools and houses sprawling lie.
The Citadel's faint form is lost as night falls
The lights on bridge and hills and shore appear.
And wraith-like in the placid harbour waters
Are shadowed shapes of ships at every pier.

Frances C. Murray, 1967